PRAISE FOR

GOD'S PROMISE AND THE FUTURE OF ISRAEL

God's Promise and the Future of Israel is dynamite! Vintage Don!
It is clear, personal, articulate and fun to read, and it will raise your sights
to the coming of the reign of the Messiah and to the full redemption of
His covenant people. Don Finto is one of the most influential men in my life.
His walk with God is dynamic, personal and *life* to all who meet him.
You will discover why in this book.

TOD BELL

Author, *It Can Be Done: The Marketplace Maximized for the Kingdom of God*
Midsouth Regional Director, Harvest Evangelism
Founder, New Vision Network and Pass the Salt Marketplace Luncheons

Don Finto is a rare breed of Christian leader. A successful pastor of
Belmont Church in Nashville (where I first met him), Don hasn't
rested on his laurels, but has "retired" into an entirely different and
critically important ministry, namely that of promoting God's work
among the Jewish people today. Don's abiding love for Israel has not
diminished his desire to see Jewish people come to Christ or distance
himself from Jews who come to faith in Christ. Instead, Don has
developed close ties to the Messianic Jewish movement. *God's Promise
and the Future of Israel* grows out of these convictions and provides
information that is helpful for Christians who want to understand
what God is doing today among Messianic Jews and in the land of Israel.

DAVID BRICKNER

Executive Director, Jews for Jesus

If you're involved in worldwide evangelism, *God's Promise and the Future of Israel* is a must-read. In this book, Don explains and defends the idea that nations come to know Jesus as God through His dealings with Israel. You will see how God is fulfilling the ancient prophecies right now in Israel and what this means to the Gentile Church. As a marketplace minister, I'm excited after reading this book about being engaged in ministries in businesses in Israel. Read this book and find out why.

MIKE FRANK

President, Frank Consulting
Santa Barbara, California

In *God's Promise and the Future of Israel,* Don Finto has given us one of the most helpful roadmaps toward a biblical understanding of God's purposes for the people of Israel. With stunning clarity, he offers insightful answers to the questions surrounding Israel's place in the heart of God, why the chosen people are still the chosen people, and why we need to stand in a posture of blessing toward Israel. *God's Promise and the Future of Israel* is penetrating in its analysis and balanced in its presentation.

STEVEN L. FRY

Senior Pastor, Belmont Church
Nashville, Tennessee

Above the noise currently surrounding subjects such as the nation of Israel, the Jewish people, the Middle East and biblical prophecy comes the clear, calm and compassionate voice of Don Finto. Don speaks with the fiery passion of a prophet, the careful skill of a scholar and the gentle concern of a pastor. In *God's Promise and the Future of Israel,* Don offers insights, answers questions and presents challenges to all, Jew and non-Jew alike, who wrestle with these timely and essential issues.

MARTY GOETZ

Messianic Music Minister

With the art of a statesman, Don Finto communicates "loud and clear" for all to hear the relevant message of God's promise for Israel and the Jewish people. Solid answers for perplexing questions fill the pages of this strategic read. Clear the fog by reading this book!

JAMES W. GOLL

Cofounder, Encounters Network
Author, *The Seer* and *Praying for Israel's Destiny*

Pulsing with God's heartbeat for His chosen people, *God's Promise and the Future of Israel* brings further revelation to the Body of Christ concerning the prophetic purposes for the people and land of Israel. In this book, Don traces biblically the history-altering events that occurred when the promise of God intersected with the timing of God—a "suddenly" that changed the course of nations—and then outlines with clarity and revelation the "suddenlies" that are happening in our current day and their significance in the plan of God. Don's answers to questions that often arise concerning Israel and the Jewish people bring insight and understanding to some of the pertinent issues in the Israeli/Arab struggle. A must-read for every believer.

JANE HANSEN
President and Chief Executive Officer, Aglow International

There is no more discerning perspective than Don Finto's when we seek to grasp God's profound dealings with the Jewish people or the nation of Israel today. Any reader, Jew or Gentile, will profit by this book, and every Christian leader deserves to have the answers to the forthright questions it addresses.

JACK W. HAYFORD
President, International Foursquare Church
Chancellor, The King's College and Seminary
Los Angeles, California

Don Finto's new book, *God's Promise and the Future of Israel*, is both thought provoking and biblical. In this book, Don presents a wealth of material that he has gleaned over years of faithful ministry to the Body of Christ and by means of his "hands on" relationship with Israel and her people. I deeply appreciate the manner in which Don connects Israel's journey to that of the nations. Israel was always birthed with the nations in view and this has not changed. This is what the future is all about.

MALCOLM HEDDING
Executive Director, International Christian Embassy Jerusalem

Don Finto is a father to many of us who are leaders in the Messianic Jewish movement. He is a man with a passion for God's purposes for Israel and for the salvation of the nations. Yet Don's passion is tempered by clear and realistic thinking. *God's Promise and the Future of Israel* is inspirational, practical and balanced.

DANIEL JUSTER, TH.D.
Director, Tikkun International

Thank you, Don, for this comprehensive, refreshing guidebook through the really "hot" questions we're all asking about Israel. Your years of passionate pastoral ministry combined with your devoted affection for the peoples of this Land bring both sense and sensitivity to the most crucial yet often misunderstood issues concerning the mystery that is Israel. We love you.

DAVID AND MICHAELLA LAZARUS
Beit Immanuel Congregation
Netanya, Israel

Don Finto has the ability to engage your mind, ignite your heart and compel your feet to walk as "one new man" embracing the King of the Jews and the King of the Nations. *God's Promise and the Future of Israel* is captivating, educational and inspirational. It holds the keys to global revival, unity in the body of Messiah and understanding the end times, and it is relevant to people of all cultures, generations and denominations. As a gentile who longs to see the fulfillment of the great commission in all nations, the revelation that Don brings through this book is essential. I wholeheartedly recommend this book.

TOD MCDOWELL
Founder, Ignite Ministries
Missionary, Youth With A Mission
Spiritual Elder, University of the Nations in Kona, Hawaii

Five years ago, on an airplane to Harrisburg, Pennsylvania, revelation struck as Don shared with me many of the teachings found in this book. Though I had acquired two university degrees in Biblical studies, it was as if I were reading certain passages of the Bible for the very first time. I could not believe I had not seen God's promises regarding the everlasting covenant He made with the Jewish people. Since that time, these words have been the source of life and blessing for both me and the church I serve. I recommend *God's Promise and the Future of Israel* to you wholeheartedly, for I am convinced the tremendous blessings we have seen as a church over the past five years are due in large part to honoring the prophetic principle of going "first to the Jew, then to the Gentile."

DAVID MCQUEEN
Pastor, Beltway Park Baptist Church
Abilene, Texas

God's Promise and the Future of Israel is a book that everyone must read. Don has a deep insight into God's heart and an understanding of God's purposes for Israel and the Middle East. He is a man of prayer and a father to many Messianic believers in the land of Israel. As a native and local Israeli pastor, I highly recommend this book. It will inspire and bring revelation to receive God's impartation in these last days. Definitely this is a timely book "for such a time as this."

AVI MIZRACHI
Pastor, Adonai Roi (The Lord is my Shepherd) Congregation
Director, Dugit Messianic Outreach Centre
Tel Aviv, Israel

As an Israeli Messianic Jew, I strongly recommend this book. Don Finto is not writing theoretically. He is giving his life to walk with us in the Messianic movement as a devoted father. His passionate heart is uniquely knit with both the Gentile and the Jewish disciples of Yeshua. Here you will find urgently needed insights rooted in humility.

EITAN SHISHKOFF
Tents of Mercy

Years ago I recorded an instrumental song titled "Hope of Israel." Many people who heard it said there was meaning behind each note. There was, but for me, as one who has come to love the nation of Israel and the Jewish people, the emotion went beyond words. Don Finto—my pastor of many years and my mentor—has captured the essence of the hope of Israel in the book you now hold in your hands. He never just shoots the breeze—he aims for the heart of the matter and hits his target. He has done it again, challenging me (and every Christian). I probably learned the most about worship from Don Finto. Now I am learning from him the most about having a passion for Jewish people and loving them with the love of Christ.

MICHAEL W. SMITH

Don Finto is one of the most unique servants of God I know—a man of deep compassion and integrity and extraordinary strategic wisdom. If only every Christian leader and dedicated lay person would read this book! It unlocks key end time signs and their significance for you and your life mission. Understanding God's strategy and timing revealed in this book will make a huge difference in your personal and corporate spiritual harvest.

ARI SORKO-RAM
President, Maoz Israel Ministries

God has filled Don Finto's heart with a passion for the Body of Christ to enter our full destiny, which means we must understand and participate in God's purposes for Israel and the Jewish people. In this articulate and persuasive book, Don informs us clearly, step by step, the Biblical basis for this stance. The one who engages this work with an open heart will not remain the same. You will be motivated to action . . . read at your own risk!

ROBERT STEARNS
Founder, Eagles' Wings Ministries
Author, *Prepare the Way*

God's Promise and the Future of Israel is truly anointed! It is a book to be read and read again by one of the foremost biblical scholars of our time. Study these words, keep a copy for your library and purchase additional copies to pass on to friends and family and church.

BROCK AND BODIE THOENE
Authors, The Zion Covenant Series, The Shiloh Legacy Series, and The A.D. Chronicles Series

GOD'S PROMISE
AND THE
FUTURE OF ISRAEL

DON FINTO

Regal

From Gospel Light
Ventura, California, U.S.A.

PUBLISHED BY REGAL BOOKS
FROM GOSPEL LIGHT
VENTURA, CALIFORNIA, U.S.A.
PRINTED IN THE U.S.A.

Regal Books is a ministry of Gospel Light, a Christian publisher dedicated to serving the local church. We believe God's vision for Gospel Light is to provide church leaders with biblical, user-friendly materials that will help them evangelize, disciple and minister to children, youth and families.

It is our prayer that this Regal book will help you discover biblical truth for your own life and help you meet the needs of others. May God richly bless you.

For a free catalog of resources from Regal Books/Gospel Light, please call your Christian supplier or contact us at 1-800-4-GOSPEL or www.regalbooks.com.

Library of Congress Cataloging-in-Publication Data
Finto, Don, 1930-
    God's promise and the future of Israel / Don Finto.
    p. cm.
    Includes bibliographical references.
    ISBN 0-8307-3811-8 (trade paper)
    1. Israel (Christian theology) 2. Jewish Christians.   I. Title.
BT93.F56 2005
231.7'6—dc22   2005019286

1   2   3   4   5   6   7   8   9   10   /   10   09   08   07   06   05

Rights for publishing this book in other languages are contracted by Gospel Light Worldwide, the international nonprofit ministry of Gospel Light. Gospel Light Worldwide also provides publishing and technical assistance to international publishers dedicated to producing Sunday School and Vacation Bible School curricula and books in the languages of the world. For additional information, visit www.gospellightworldwide.org; write to Gospel Light Worldwide, P.O. Box 3875, Ventura, CA 93006; or send an e-mail to info@gospellightworldwide.org.

CONTENTS

PART 1:
"THE TIME HAS COME"

Jesus, on the night that He was betrayed, broke bread with His disciples and prayed, "Father, the time has come." The time has also come for the Jewish people to return as a nation to the world scene, a historical fact that is affecting our world.

Biblical examples of God's intervention, when His promise and His timing have intersected in the past, provide evidence of God's faithfulness and point to the ways in which promise and timing are intersecting in our day.

The return of Israel is the most significant biblically predicted event of the last two thousand years of world history—all in God's timing.

Nineteen years after the rebirth of the nation, God accentuated that return through the Six-Day War of 1967, when Israel reclaimed her ancient capital in Jerusalem, all according to promise.

The Messianic Jewish movement, no longer hidden, is a viable growing organism both in Israel and throughout the world—another present-day fulfillment of Scripture.

The astounding growth of the Church in Africa, Asia and Latin America is bringing about a shift of the Church's power from the West. This revival in the nations is part of Paul's and Ezekiel's visions of the end times.

As unconditional love for the Church's "elder brother," Israel, replaces fear, mistrust, hatred and suspicion, individual Christians are able to do much to support and encourage Jewish people, both believers and nonbelievers. Guidelines for action and personal testimonies will help you determine the ways in which you, too, can make a difference at this critical time in world history.

A Personal Word from Don Finto

I grew up with a certain reverence for the Bible, but it was not until more recent years that I have been motivated to read it for the sheer joy of drawing near to God and knowing Him better. In recent decades I have become increasingly aware of the importance of biblical prophecy. The constant threat of nuclear war, the reality of international terrorism and the proliferation of films and books that paint potential catastrophic possibilities and depict end-of-the-world scenarios compel all of us to think about the future.

So many people who are seeking answers today reach out to "spirit guides," consult astrology charts or try to read tea leaves or tarot cards in order to find out more about God. We travel to the East to study under shamans. We read Nostradamus and Edgar Cayce, the Veda, the Koran, Bhagavad Gita and the Tao Te Ching to gain insights into our times. We have our Big Bang theories and end-of-the-world hypotheses, but we rarely refer to this ancient Book called the Bible. Sometimes we have gained the impression, perhaps through a radio or television evangelist, that the Bible causes us to hate each other rather than to love, narrows our view of life, and makes bigots of us all.

Even many of us who say that we believe the Bible, who frequent worship assemblies with some regularity and who consider ourselves born again, have never once read the Bible in its entirety and do not consider the possibility that this ancient book of writings, purported to have come from God's chosen scribes, is often an excellent commentary on current events.

I want to encourage you to reconsider all this and to pull out the old family Bible (or go to the bookstore and buy one) and begin to read it. The Lord has promised that He will reveal Himself to those who seek Him. The biblical prophets spoke often of our day. Moses lived about 3,500 years ago; Isaiah, Jeremiah, Daniel and the Hebrew prophets more than 2,400 years ago. Yet their predictions often describe our times with amazing accuracy. Do not let your view of Christians and of the Church limit your ability to hear from God. Read in order to learn, not to prove what you already believe!

To my Jewish friends: If you have not picked up the *Tanakh* (Old Testament) lately, I would encourage you to do so. You will find there some *very interesting* prophecies about the nation of Israel. Moses, Isaiah, Jeremiah, Ezekiel and the other prophets lived 2,000 to 3,000 years ago, and yet they spoke clearly of our day, when Israel would return from the nations.

Read the history of your people—especially the Prophets. You will not understand everything, even if you are a major historian. But you will find many passages that describe the history of the Jewish people up to the time of the scattering of the Northern tribes under Assyria, the exile and return under Babylon, the dispersion into the nations after the destruction of the temple in A.D. 70, and the present-day return to the Land.

There are also those equally thought-provoking and inspired words about a Man, a Redeemer, a Messiah who would come, a descendant of David. (I do understand that there is disagreement today within the Jewish community about whether we should still expect a personal Messiah, but read the Scriptures for yourself. *You* decide.)

A growing number of Jewish people around the world are beginning to believe that Christians and Jews should be much closer to each other. We have many things in common. Both see Abraham as the father of their faith. Both agree that the Ten Commandments and even the moral laws of the Jewish Scripture are essential for living life to the fullest. Could it be that the Christian "Jesus" and the Jewish Messiah are the same person?

You may want to read some of the Messianic prophecies and see if you think they could possibly refer to Jesus. Isaiah 53 sounds strangely like the suffering and crucified Lord of the Gospels. Isaiah 9 speaks of the birth of a Son who would be called "Mighty God, Everlasting Father, Prince of Peace" (v. 6). Moses assured all future generations that, after the scattering to the nations, "if from there you seek the LORD your God, you will find him if you look for him with all your heart and with all your soul" (Deut. 4:29). You, my friends, are a part of those future generations. Your God, your prophets, and your Bible have promised you that if you will seek God with all your heart, you will find Him.

Do not allow the Church's horrific history against the Jewish people to affect the way you hear from God. More and more of us non-Jews are developing a growing love for the Jewish family of faith and are determined to stand with you, whether or not we ever agree. After all, we share the same biblical heritage. As one of my friends says, "It is your family journal that has become our Sacred Scripture."

ACKNOWLEDGMENTS

How could I have known, after years of pastoring a local congregation, that God would open up to me this world of the Jewish people? His ways really are beyond our comprehension. Thank you, Eitan and Connie, Asher and Betty, Dan and Patti, Ayal and Yardena, Ofer and Chris, Avner and Rachel, David and Emma, Marty and Marlene, Avi and Chaya, Ari and Shira, Eddie and Jackie, David and Michaela, Evan and Maala, and all of you who have let me into your hearts and who are now sealed eternally in mine. You have taught me and welcomed me as one of you.

I have had a few outstanding "encouragers" in my life. Anne Severance ranks at the top. She is more than an editor. She is a woman of God who knows how to bring more out of people than they even knew was there. I would not want to undertake any writing assignment without her.

How thankful I am for some of the recent books that have encouraged Christian leaders to have intercessors! When I hit a snag and wondered if I could go forward, I knew that Tina Marie Cerra, my faithful coworker and lover of God and of His covenant people, would rally the forces. Thank you to all of you who have believed with me, including the entire Belmont Church family who have loved us and supported us for almost 35 years. I am grateful to call Steve Fry my pastor.

And I continue to be awed that my Martha can maintain her sanity, having been married to me for more than 50 years! I often tell brides and grooms that, on that day when they take their vows, they are marrying many different people—the person who was, the person who is, and all the people that person will become! There have been many changes in my life, and Martha has been beside me the whole journey. Even when she did not understand me, she trusted my heart for God. That is huge, and I will be eternally grateful.

Gospel Light and Regal, I still love you. I love your hearts. I love the reason for your existence—get His message out! Bill III, Bill II, Kim and Roger, be blessed!

And now "to the King eternal, immortal, invisible, the only God, be honor and glory for ever and ever. Amen" (1 Tim. 1:17).

INTRODUCTION

Just recently, after spending time with a group of pastors in one of our nation's northern states, two brothers stayed behind to inquire more about the several hundred thousand Jewish people who have come to faith in Jesus as their Messiah in the last 30 to 35 years. It was an interesting encounter as we talked together. I could almost see the wheels turning in their heads as they tried to find a box into which to fit this startling information.

Their theological training had taught them that the Church would be taken to heaven before the Jewish people came to faith, and yet I was telling them that 400,000 or more of these first-covenant people have come to believe in Jesus in the last decades. I found myself almost grateful for my lack of higher theological training[1] since I had fewer preconceived notions about how God would bring about the return of the Jewish people and about other end-time biblical predictions.

My involvement with the Messianic Jewish movement began when many Jewish young people turned to faith during the Jesus Movement of the late 1960s and early 1970s; some of them became "my sheep." Of course I did not know how to shepherd them, because it was all too new to me; so I had to take a crash course in "Jewishness." At least I was wise enough to reach out to some who were far ahead of me on the road—Dan Juster, Andrew (Eitan) Shishkoff, Keith (Asher) Intrater and others. I became acquainted with Jews for Jesus, Chosen People, Liberated Wailing Wall, Lamb, and other Jewish believers in Jesus who were trying to find their way in a totally Gentile Christian environment.

Today the number of Jewish believers has risen dramatically. It is no longer strange to find Jewish people who believe in *Yeshua*

(Jesus) as their Messiah. The son of one of our well-known Jewish doctors in town came to faith through Jews for Jesus. Another physician himself became a believer, much to the dismay of his family. According to recent surveys, in Israel there are now about 120 different house groups or synagogues of "Messianic believers," some having as many as 300 members.[2]

The old Histadrut (Labor) headquarters of David ben Gurion in Tel Aviv is now a Messianic center with the Dugit Bookstore and Outreach Center on the ground floor, where a number of congregations (of different ethnic groups) meet for worship. The largest old theater in downtown Jerusalem has been bought and renovated as a community center for believers. It will be used for congregational meetings, concerts, drama and all sorts of ministry. Not far from that location are an innovative media-production center and music coffee house, which reach out to a young generation of Israelis.

A house, once purchased by the Anglican community in old Joppa, has now been turned over to Beit Immanuel Messianic congregation, which serves the growing body of believers in the area, including many of Russian descent. An Amharic-speaking, Ethiopian congregation and an Arab congregation use the building as well. The former Stella Carmel guesthouse on Mount Carmel, run by the Anglicans for years, is now owned and operated by a Messianic congregation that reaches out to both Jews and Arabs. Christ Church, in the Old City of Jerusalem, has a Hebrew-speaking congregation as well as an English-speaking one.

No fewer than 100 Messianic believers now serve in the Israeli army, some as officers. The former head of the Jewish Agency in a very prominent city in Eastern Europe is now a believer and helps to lead congregations both in the *Diaspora* (Jewish people living outside of Israel) and in Israel. In a northern Israeli city, the mayor and government officials have expressed appreciation to the Messianic congregations for humanitarian aid and other types of aid and have welcomed a new Messianic congregation to their city.

In 2001, I wrote my first book, *Your People Shall Be My People.* Two primary reasons compelled me to write it. First, the Church as a whole seemed to know little of the growing Messianic Jewish movement, even though there are several hundred congregations in the United States, the former Soviet Union, Europe, Latin America and Israel. Some are small home meetings; others are quite large. The largest Messianic congregation in the world is in Kiev, Ukraine, with a weekly attendance of more than 1,400.

Second, I knew of no one who had connected world revival to the return of Israel to the Land and to the Lord, even though the Bible clearly indicates that we will experience "greater riches" when "their fullness" occurs (see Rom. 11:12), that it will be "life from the dead" when they begin to accept Messiah (see Rom. 11:15) and that the nations will know the Lord when He shows Himself powerful through Israel in the eyes of the whole world (see Ezek. 36:23).

The publication of *Your People Shall Be My People* has opened up many doors of ministry. Translations in German, French, Dutch and Russian also keep our e-mail and telephone communications busy. I have spoken to a gathering of Pentecostal pastors in Italy and traveled across Australia and New Zealand. The English translation was given to 10,000 pastors and leaders at the 2003 Phoenix, Arizona, Promise Keepers Pastors' Gathering, to the leaders of Youth with a Mission in their Singapore meeting the same year, as well as to denominational leaders as they gathered in various locations.

I have met with leaders from about 70 nations at Tom Hess's All Nations Prayer Convocation in Jerusalem, followed by the annual

Feast of Tabernacles celebration sponsored by the International Christian Embassy, Jerusalem, whose representation includes almost 100 nations. Doors have opened for meetings with leaders in the Jewish community, with representatives from the Consul General in Atlanta and then, later, with the Consul General from Ottawa, Canada.

In all of these settings, many questions have arisen. Some I thought I could answer; others were not so easy. Some answers were encouraging; others were disappointing. The Lord still continues to bring revelation, and yet the questions asked still call for an answer.

Shortly after the publication of *Your People Shall Be My People,* I began to see our present-day scenario—the reestablishment of the State of Israel in 1948, the retaking of Jerusalem in the Six-Day War of June 1967, the opening of Jewish eyes to the message of Jesus, the revivals around the world and the increasing awareness of many of us in the Church regarding the Jewish roots of our faith—as an intersection of God's promises with God's timing.

These thoughts bring us to the dual purpose of this book: (1) to look at the intersection of promise and timing in our day, and (2) to provide answers to questions about Israel and the Jewish people.

But as you read all this, remember that it's not really about Israel! It's not even about revival among the nations. It is about a God who loves and who comes to free us to be who we were created to be. It is about a forever-loving, covenant-keeping God. That's why Israel comes in as a visible reminder of the God who does not forget—even after 2,000 years. He is still there—waiting, loving, wooing. And yes, Israel will again be a blessing and a light to all the nations.

This book has much to say about Israel and God's purposes with and through her, but it's also about you. He calls you, not because He needs you, but because you need Him. That God-shaped vacuum within you will know peace only as you rest in Him and He in you.

Notes

1. I obtained my Ph.D. in German literature from Vanderbilt University in Nashville, Tennessee, after which I became head of the language department at Lipscomb University. I also have an M.A. with an emphasis in counseling from Harding Graduate School of Religion in Memphis, Tennessee, and I received further Bible training from an institution that is now Abilene Christian University in Abilene, Texas. None of these degrees or diplomas, however, granted me training as a theologian.

2. According to Kai Kjaer-Hansen and Bodil F. Skjott in their book *Facts and Myths About the Messianic Congregations in Israel* (Jerusalem, Israel: United Christian Council in Israel in cooperation with the Caspari Center for Biblical and Jewish Studies, 1999, p. 12), there were 81 congregations and house groups of Messianic believers meeting in Israel at the time of the book's publication. Current surveys conducted by Tom Hess indicate that the number is upward of 120.

PART I
"THE TIME HAS COME"

Jesus spoke these words shortly before His death. Jesus lived to die.

Early in His public ministry, Jesus said, "My time has not yet come" (John 2:4). On another occasion, when His brothers were preparing to go to Jerusalem for the Feast of Tabernacles, they asked Him whether He also planned to go. "The right time for me has not yet come" was His answer (7:6).

But on the night of His betrayal, Jesus said to His disciples, "My appointed time is near" (Matt. 26:18). And in one of His last prayers, Jesus "looked up toward heaven and prayed, *'Father, the time has come'*" (John 17:1, emphasis added).

When Paul later reflected on the life of Jesus, he wrote to the Galatians, "But when the time had fully come, God sent his Son" (4:4), and to the Romans, "You see, at just the right time, . . . Christ died for the ungodly" (5:6).

The time has come in our world as well, the time to which many of the prophets pointed. Get out your Bibles—for you, my Jewish friends, your Tanakh—and let's look at the prophetic season in which we find ourselves.

WHEN PROMISE AND
TIMING INTERSECT

But when the time had fully come, God sent his Son,
born of a woman, born under law, to redeem those under law,
that we might receive the full rights of sons.

GALATIANS 4:4

When the promise of God and the timing of God intersect, there is a "suddenly" that causes a significant change in the world, and God begins to look for people who will participate with Him in what He is doing in that generation.

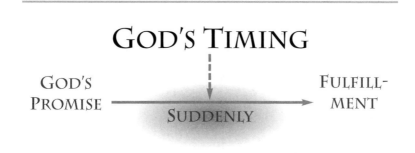

Moses and the burning bush. Joshua and the priests' setting foot in the Jordan. The Jewish leaders' return from Babylon in the days of Daniel the prophet. Gabriel's appearance to Zechariah in the temple. The founding of the State of Israel in 1948. Jerusalem's returning to Israeli control after the Six-Day War of June 1967. What do all these events have in common? They mark the intersection of God's promise with God's timing.

A PROMISE GIVEN

For 400 years the descendants of Jacob had languished in a foreign country. The early years had been good years. Jacob's son,

Joseph, was the prime minister of Egypt, confidant of the Pharaoh; as a result, Jacob's other sons and their tribes had been granted some of the best pastureland in the country. But that condition changed rapidly after the death of Joseph.

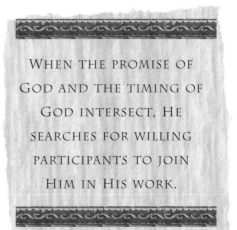

WHEN THE PROMISE OF GOD AND THE TIMING OF GOD INTERSECT, HE SEARCHES FOR WILLING PARTICIPANTS TO JOIN HIM IN HIS WORK.

For centuries the children of Israel had been considered the scum of Egypt. On their backs the great Egyptian structures were built. The promise given to their father Abraham about being a nation of their own in their country of origin was like an indistinct legend. God's words had been clear enough when first spoken to Abraham:

> Know for certain that your descendants will be strangers in a country not their own, and they will be enslaved and mistreated four hundred years. But I will punish the nation they serve as slaves, and afterward they will come out with great possessions (Gen. 15:13-14).

The promise was clear—I will bring you back. The timing was settled—in 400 years. But Egypt was the mightiest empire in the world. How could the promise come to pass when the enslavement of Abraham's descendants seemed so permanent?

And then one day, a bush burned in a Midianite desert. God encountered a man. That burning bush was the "suddenly" of Moses' generation, indicating that the landscape of the nations was about to change. God's promise and God's timing intersected at the bush. He was searching for willing participants to join Him in His work in that time.

Moses, the reluctant leader, returned to Egypt to begin the confrontations with Pharaoh and his Egyptian court. At first, things seemed not to go well. Egyptian magicians matched the work of God. Moses' rod-turned-snake consumed the rod of Pharaoh's sorcerers, but it appeared to be an unsuccessful conflict of powers. Pharaoh made promises but then refused to honor them. The Egyptian taskmasters became even more demanding. The whole nation of Israel grew disillusioned and angry with Moses and Aaron, the very men who carried the message of God.

But the following years proved that there had, indeed, been a God-encounter. No generation had ever experienced what was about to take place. No guidelines were written. It was necessary to listen for God every step of the way—and to be obedient. God was fulfilling His promise. His people were being set free. Many frustrating years lay ahead, ignominious defeats along with miraculous victories, but an irreversible course had been set. God's promise to Abraham was not to be denied. Promise and timing had intersected.

CROSSING THE JORDAN

"For forty years—one year for each of the forty days you explored the land—you will suffer for your sins and know what it is like to have me against you" (Num. 14:34), God told Israel after they rejected the counsel of Caleb and Joshua and refused to go up and conquer their enemies. The promise was confirmed—you will yet enter the Land. The timing was given—after 40 years. Every adult male, with the exception of those two faithful men, was buried in the desert before God would allow Joshua to lead the nation into the Land promised to Abraham's descendants. Israel suffered through the miseries of their nomadic existence—2 million people eating manna each day, never sure how long they would tarry in any one location. The punishment for their disbelief took its toll on an entire generation. Not until after the death of Moses and Aaron did Joshua hear the words from the Lord:

> Get ready to cross the Jordan River into the land I am about to give to them. As soon as the priests who carry the ark of the LORD—the Lord of all the earth—set foot in the Jordan, its water flowing downstream will be cut off and stand up in a heap (Josh. 1:2; 3:13).

When the 40 years ended, the whole nation and all nations surrounding were forever changed. The divided water was the sign that promise and timing had intersected again.

RETURN FROM BABYLON

The promise came through the prophet Jeremiah in the days when the Babylonian king Nebuchadnezzar invaded Jerusalem, destroyed the Temple and carried the king and the leading officials in Jerusalem into Babylonian exile. "When seventy years are completed for Babylon, I will come to you and fulfill my gracious promise to bring you back to this place" (Jer. 29:10). Captivity for 70 years and then the return—that was the prophetic prediction.

Among the early captives to Babylon, young Daniel, who was trained to enter the king's service, proved himself to be so valuable to the king that he was later promoted to a position over all of the wise men in the province (see Dan. 2:48). One day, many years later, after Daniel had become an old man, he was reading in the Jeremiah scroll and came across the prophet's words that promised the return. Daniel understood that he was living in the time for the promise to be fulfilled, so he began to give himself to prayer and fasting for that return (see 9:2-3). The old prophet came to God in intercessory prayer, taking upon himself the sins of kings and princes long since dead and crying out to God for mercy and for the fulfillment of the promise (see 9:4-8,17-19). Later, in recounting the story, Scripture says that Daniel "remained there [in Babylon] until the first year of King Cyrus" (1:21), indicating that Daniel was among those who participated with God as His promise and His timing intersected and the exiles were brought home.

IN THE FULLNESS OF TIME

For 4,000 years the promise of God to Eve in the Garden—that the seed of the woman would crush the serpent's head (see Gen. 3:15)—lay dormant among the folklore of an erratic and often schizophrenic nation. The mysteriously worded promise would sometimes take on momentary, veiled assurance as prophets arose and spoke of a coming Redeemer. A remnant of Israel held on to those promises tenaciously; others seemed to move carelessly forward while the nation suffered through the oppression of world empires that surrounded and plagued her: Assyria, Babylon, Persia, Greece and Rome. Life's circumstances left little time for prophetic dreams. Long intervals passed without reference to the coming Chosen One.

All that changed one day when Zechariah went into the Temple to perform his normal priestly duties. After centuries of waiting in expectation, a strange thing happened. During the daily incense offering, an angel appeared at the right side of the altar (see Luke 1:11). The angel announced that Zechariah's aged wife, Elizabeth, was to give birth to a son who would prepare the way for the Messiah. Zechariah's inability to speak until after the birth of his son John was evidence to the gathered crowd and to his friends that something unusual had happened in the Temple—God's stunning announcement that His promised Messiah was about to appear. The promises of centuries were about to intersect with the timing of God.

Rumors must have swirled around young Miriam (Mary) a few months later when she found herself pregnant before her marriage to Joseph. How could this be?! She had not been intimate with any man. But even stranger things unfolded in the following months.

On the night of her son's birth, shepherds in the surrounding fields spoke of angels who had appeared and had directed them to the young child. Wise men from the east came, inquiring of the king who was to be born. When King Herod heard of the visit, he began to ask the chief priest and teachers of the law where the infant Messiah could be found. "In Bethlehem of Judea" was their reply (Matt. 2:5).

That all of this took place at the precise time the prophet Daniel had predicted the Anointed One would come (see Dan. 2:44; 9:25) should have alerted every reader of Scripture. Yet it all seems to have been forgotten by the time Jesus, as an adult, began to teach and minister with such authority, evidenced by the miraculous signs that accompanied Him.

"When the time had fully come" (Gal. 4:4), Rabbi Shaul (the apostle Paul) wrote many years later when thinking back on all that had transpired during those prophecy-fulfilling, world-changing days.

The appearance of the angel Gabriel to Zechariah, then later to Miriam (Mary) in Nazareth, was the "suddenly" that announced to all Israel and ultimately to the world, that the promises of the generations were about to find their fulfillment. It would still be 30 years before John would make his appearance in the wilderness of Judea and Jesus would begin His brief three years of public ministry, but an irreversible course had been set. God's promise to Eve in the Garden and His assurances to Isaiah, Micah and the prophets would soon come to pass. The promise of God and the timing of God had intersected. The world was forever changed. Thereafter, in every period of history, God would be looking for those who would participate with Him in His work.

THE TIME OF THE MESSIAH'S RETURN IS NEAR. ISRAEL IS BACK IN THE LAND. GOD'S PROMISE AND TIMING HAVE INTERSECTED IN OUR DAY.

PROMISES KEPT

Today we stand at another intersection of promise and timing. Within the past 60 years, two historical events have brought about the fulfillment of biblical promises and have changed the course of the nations.

1. The birth of the State of Israel in May 1948, resulting from the United Nations' vote in November 1947, was God's announcement to a watching world that major world shifts were about to take place—that the

time of the Messiah's return is near. Israel is back. Promise and timing have intersected *in our day.*

2. The recapture of Jerusalem by the nation of Israel during the Six-Day War in June 1967 was God's exclamation point that His plans were on schedule. King David's capital city is back in Israel's possession, just as Jesus Himself foretold (see Luke 21:24).

These two events have triggered three other phenomena that are having an impact on our world with exponential force.

1. Hundreds of thousands of Jewish people have opened their hearts to believe that Yeshua (Jesus) is indeed the Messiah of Israel, just as Isaiah, Hosea, Ezekiel and others predicted. Not since the first century, when the original Church was totally Jewish, have so many Jewish people begun to believe that Jesus is the long-awaited, prophecy-foretold Messiah of Israel.

2. An expansion of faith in this Jewish Messiah is reaching around the world to shake nations that have long known nothing of the world's Redeemer—exactly as Paul foresaw when writing to the Romans, just as the prophet Ezekiel had predicted and just as prophecy students have come to believe in the past 400 years or more.

3. The Church throughout the world is becoming aware of her own Jewish heritage and her "grafted-in-ness" to the family of Israel, and is becoming united as the "one new man" of which Paul spoke in Ephesians 2:15. Sadly, the Church has not been kind to the Jewish people through the centuries. All that is changing in our day, as fresh revelation about the Jewish roots of our

faith reaches the ends of the earth and as the Church grows in her desire to affirm and bless the people of the Land.

Let us take a more careful look at each of these intersections before we begin to answer some of the questions they evoke.

THE REBIRTH OF THE NATION OF ISRAEL

I will take you out of the nations; I will gather you from all the countries and bring you back into your own land.

EZEKIEL 36:24

On May 24 and 25, 1991, 34 El Al C-130 Hercules airlifted 14,325 Ethiopian Jews from Addis Ababa to Tel Aviv in the well-executed Operation Solomon.[1] Seats were removed from the aircraft to maximize passenger capacity. According to Pastor Gerald Gotzen, who had worked in Ethiopia since the days of Emperor Haile Selassie, there was one particular plane in which passengers were meticulously counted as they left Addis Ababa, only to find upon arrival at Ben-Gurion Airport in Israel that the passenger count had increased by 10. Ten babies had been born during the flight!

Twenty-five hundred years earlier, when Jeremiah was describing Israel's return from the nations to which they had been dispersed, he predicted this Ethiopian airlift with astonishing specificity. "Among them," Jeremiah said of the returning exiles, "will be the blind and the lame, expectant mothers and *women in labor*" (31:8, emphasis added).

In March 2003, Curt Landry, a Jewish believer in Jesus,[2] and I traveled to New Zealand to challenge the Church in its relationship with this covenant people of God. Not until we were well into our visit to this nation did we realize that we were doing exactly what Jeremiah had advised us to do: "Proclaim it in distant coastlands: 'He who scattered Israel will gather them and will watch over his flock like a shepherd'" (31:10). New Zealand is the most distant "coastland" from Israel, exactly 12 time zones away from Jerusalem, the "center of the nations" (Ezek. 5:5). In Acts 2, Peter explains the astonishing arrival of the Spirit and the "strange behavior" of the disciples by referring to the prophecy of Joel, saying "This is that!" (v. 16, *KJV*). Curt and I were having a "This is that!" experience.

THIS IS THAT!

Steve Lightle wrote his book *Exodus II* in 1983. This was six years before the Berlin Wall came down and eight years before the collapse of Russian communism and Russia's move toward some form of democratic government.

For 10 years prior to the publication of his book, Lightle had been traveling in Europe and other nations, predicting the fall of communism and the return of the Russian Jews to Israel. This revelation had come to him from two sources: the visions and dreams that the Lord had given him and the words of the Old Testament prophets.

> The days are coming . . . when people will no longer say, "As surely as the LORD lives, who brought the Israelites up out of Egypt," but they will say, "As surely as the LORD lives, who brought the descendants of Israel up out of the land of the north and out of all the countries where he had banished them." Then they will live in their own land (Jer. 23:7-8).

"We are living in a decisive period of history in God's redemptive plan in which Jesus is preparing His church around the world for the fulfillment of another important end-time prophecy," Lightle and his coeditors wrote. "Some of the end-time prophecies have already come to pass, like the founding of the State of Israel in May of 1948 (see Isa. 66:8) and the liberation of the old city of Jerusalem in June of 1967 (see Luke 21:24), so we can expect the release of His people out of the 'country of the north' and the worldwide homecoming of the Jews into their land."[3]

Quite remarkably, within eight years of the publication of Lightle's book, the Berlin Wall came down (November 9, 1989), communism in Russia collapsed, steps were being taken toward democracy, and Russian Jews were returning from centuries of exile. Today approximately 20 percent of Israel's Jewish population (over 1 million) are Russian-speaking.

Steve Lightle and his friends (among them, my friend Curt Landry, a newcomer to the group[4]) read the Prophets and listened for God's instructions as they anticipated the coming of the Jewish people from the north.

They read Isaiah 60:8, which says, "Who are these that fly along like clouds, like doves to their nests?" and realized that the Lord wanted to use airplanes to bring back the "captives." In 1990, after the fall of the Berlin Wall but before the collapse of Russia's communist empire, Steve and his partners went to Boeing in Seattle, Washington, to inquire about the cost of leasing a Boeing 747 to fly from Moscow to Tel Aviv. One of the brothers wrote a check for the amount, thereby acquiring the first airplane used exclusively for the return of Russian Jews to the Land.

As they read on in the book of Isaiah, the very next verse brought another revelation. "Surely the islands look to me; in the lead are the ships of Tarshish, bringing your sons from afar, with their silver and gold, to the honor of the LORD your God, the Holy One of Israel" (v. 9).

"Oh," they mused. "He also wants to use ships so that those returning can bring their belongings." So in 1993, this group traveled to Greece to speak with a shipping magnate about leasing an entire ship for *aliyah* (the term used for the Jewish return to the Land).

"We do not have a ship for you," said the shipping magnate with a shrug.

"Yes, you do," returned Steve Lightle's prophetic company. "The Lord told us you have one."

"Well, we do have a ship," he admitted, "but it is not where you need it. It is not in Russia."

"Then where is it?"

"It's in Tarshish." (Tarshish is generally assumed to be Spain.)

"That is the very one we want!"

Thus, the first ship was used exclusively for these new Russian *olim* (a Hebrew word meaning "immigrants"). During the next few years, many ships would be used to bring the 1 million Russian Jews out of exile into the country of their inheritance.

LET MY PEOPLE GO!

On another continent, miles from Steve Lightle, God was stirring Kjell Sjoberg, from Stockholm, Sweden, and a group of intercessors with the urgency of time as it related to the release of the Jewish people from the north. Kjell, who has since gone on to be with the Lord, told of a meeting that took place in Stockholm in March 1982, when the Spirit of God led a group of intercessors to pray for the Jewish people in the Soviet Union. As they obeyed the voice of the Lord, they began to sense that they were to pray with authority against the spiritual powers controlling the Soviet Union. "Give up, give up, you Pharaoh of Soviet Russia!" they prayed. "In the name of Jesus Christ of Nazareth, we command you, you wild beast of the Soviet Union, let the people of God go, for the time has come for God's people to leave the Soviet Union!" They prayed for Brezhnev's successor, not knowing that, only eight months later, Brezhnev would die and that, less than 10 years later, a massive Jewish exodus would begin out of the north.[5]

Our day was seen prophetically long before there was any knowledge of communism, long before there was a Russia or a United States of America. Isaiah spoke 700 years before the birth of Jesus; Jeremiah and Ezekiel, over 500 years prior to His coming. Both foresaw a time when the sons of Israel, who had been exiled to the nations, would be brought back to their homeland and a nation would be reborn.

Isaiah spoke of a nation's being born in a day (see 66:8), foreseeing the United Nations' vote in 1947 and Israel's declaration of independence in May 1948. Isaiah, Jeremiah, Ezekiel and Hosea all spoke of the unified nation when Ephraim, the northern kingdom, and Judah, the southern kingdom, would be reunited (see Isa. 11:13; Jer. 3:18; Ezek. 37:1-17,21-22; Hos. 1:11). Jeremiah knew that this present return of over 5 million people would eclipse the 2 million-plus who returned from Egypt during the time of Moses (see Jer. 16:14-15). According to Exodus 12:37, there were 600,000 men, "besides women and children," who left the land of bondage to go home to the Promised Land.

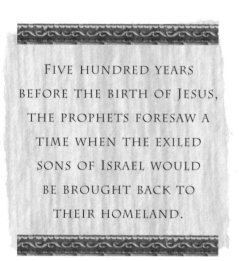

FIVE HUNDRED YEARS BEFORE THE BIRTH OF JESUS, THE PROPHETS FORESAW A TIME WHEN THE EXILED SONS OF ISRAEL WOULD BE BROUGHT BACK TO THEIR HOMELAND.

OPENING THE GRAVES OF EXILE

To serious Bible readers, the rebirth of the nation of Israel came as no surprise. For 400 years, a remnant of the Church had begun to believe that Israel would be restored to their Land before the return of the Lord. They heard the words of Jesus, which indicated an ultimate return (see Luke 21:24), and they read Ezekiel's vision of the dry bones, through which the Lord specifically said,

Son of man, these bones are the whole house of Israel. They say, "Our bones are dried up and our hope is gone; we are cut off." Therefore prophesy and say to them: "This is what the Sovereign LORD says: O my people, I am going to open your graves and bring you up from them; I will bring you back to the land of Israel. Then you, my people, will know that I am the LORD, when I open your graves and bring you up from them. I will put my Spirit in you and you will live, and I will settle you in your own land. Then you will know that I the LORD have spoken, and I have done it, declares the LORD" (Ezek. 37:11-14).

✡ The renowned nineteenth-century Baptist preacher Charles Spurgeon was certain that the Jewish people would be gathered in before the return of the Lord. In a sermon in 1871, he declared, "The day shall yet come when the Jews, who were the first apostles to the Gentiles, the first missionaries to us who were afar off, shall be gathered in again. Until that shall be, the fullness of the church's glory can never come."[6]

Today when you visit Jerusalem's Old City, you will find, just inside the Jaffa Gate, a well-known Anglican church called Christ Church that was built in anticipation of the imminent return of the Jewish people to their homeland. The dedication of the new building was in 1849, almost 100 years before the founding of the State of Israel.

This belief in the future return of the Jewish nation remained strong for the next 70 years and was the background of the Balfour Declaration in November 1917. The words of this declaration were carefully crafted, calling for "the establishment in Palestine of a national home *for* the Jewish people," rather than the original wording, which read, "the establishment of

Palestine *as* a national home for the Jewish people."[7]

All of Israel and what is today Jordan were intended to be the original homeland, but because of Arab pressure, the land mass was ultimately reduced (through the White Paper of 1939) from 45,000 square miles to 264 square miles.[8] Even that small portion had to be defended against all surrounding Arab states after David Ben-Gurion announced the establishment of the State of Israel in May 1948.

In spite of the fact that, through the centuries, Jewish households continued their Passover tradition, which concluded with the words "next year in Jerusalem," there was little serious Jewish interest in the reestablishment of a homeland for their people until Theodor Herzl, the secular Jewish reporter from Vienna, covered the trial of Alfred Dreyfus in Paris. When Dreyfus was falsely (as was later ascertained) convicted of treason, the crowd cried, "Kill the Jews!" This spurred Herzl to convene the first Zionist Congress meeting in Basel, Switzerland, in 1897. At the conclusion of those meetings, Herzl made this oft-quoted entry in his journal, dated September 3, 1897: "Were I to sum up the Basel Congress in a word—which I shall guard against pronouncing publicly—it would be this: At Basel I founded the Jewish State. If I said this out loud today, I would be answered by universal laughter. Perhaps in five years, and certainly in fifty, everyone will know it."[9] The United

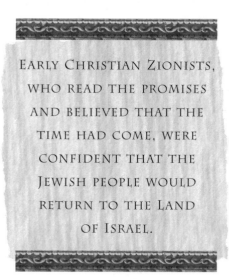

EARLY CHRISTIAN ZIONISTS, WHO READ THE PROMISES AND BELIEVED THAT THE TIME HAD COME, WERE CONFIDENT THAT THE JEWISH PEOPLE WOULD RETURN TO THE LAND OF ISRAEL.

Nations' vote that ended British control and granted the Jewish people a "reborn nation" took place on November 29, 1947—50 years and 87 days after Herzl made this statement. Herzl's words were not a prophecy; they were a plea for a safe place for his people. He was not even insistent that the place had to be their ancient homeland. The Christian Zionists, on the other hand, were confident that the Jewish people would return to the land of Israel. They had read the promises and believed that the time had come.

The promise of God and the timing of God had intersected, and prophecy students would be God's willing participants in His work to be done.

SATAN'S THRONE

The *Reichsparteitagsgelände* (Nazi Party rally grounds) in Nuremberg, Germany, was the site of many of Hitler's famous rallies. The platform from which he spoke stands atop a building that replicates the temple in ancient Pergamum. In the book of Revelation, John calls Pergamum the place "where Satan has his throne" (Rev. 2:13). In the early centuries, Pergamum was a major center for both Satan worship and emperor worship, and Christians were often taken there to test their loyalty to the caesars.[10]

Interestingly, it was also there that Hitler brought representative troops from the nation to swear loyalty to his Nazi agenda. Flags from every city were brought forward at the gatherings and ceremoniously touched to the flag that had been dipped in the blood of the 12 men who, in an early uprising, had given their lives to see the cause of Nazism succeed. Many of us who are older will remember the film clips of screaming mobs, with uplifted hands, hailing Hitler.

In 1998, when my friend Asher Intrater was invited to Nuremberg to speak, his host pastor took him to the Reichsparteitagsgelände. In Asher's inimitable style, he ascended the podium from which Hitler had spoken and proclaimed, "I want all you demons in hell to know that I am a Jew, that Hitler is gone and that we are still here!"

Not only were they still there, as Asher so boldly stated, but also they were back in their own Land and soon would be back in their ancient capital city—the one King David captured from the Jebusites in 1000 B.C.—Jerusalem.

Notes

1. The Operation Solomon airlift took its name from King Solomon, who is believed by many to have been the father of Ethiopia's Jews through the alliance of King Solomon with the Queen of Sheba. Although the truth about their alleged son may never be known, it is an historical fact that there was a Jewish population in Ethiopia several centuries before the time of Jesus.

2. Curt Landry was miraculously brought to the Lord in September 1989. Curt was a high-powered entrepreneur, with multiple homes and cars; he was a businessman who was uninterested in the things of God—until his wife, Christy, became a believer. One day, when Christy and their daughter went to visit relatives and Curt was alone in their expansive home, soaking in the Jacuzzi, he began to talk to this God in whom he did not believe: "I know that You love Christy and all her Jesus-freak friends, but if You love me, You are going to have to let me know!" Immediately a power began to surge through his body, causing him to shake and to weep uncontrollably. There seemed to be no way to turn off the power. Curt does not know how long he continued before he could get out of the tub and call his wife. "Honey, I think I've had a nervous breakdown," he moaned, to which she replied, "What happened?" When Curt began to relate his experience, she cried, "Dear, you did not have a nervous breakdown; you got saved!" And then the story began!

3. Steve Lightle, *Exodus II: Let My People Go,* with Eberhard Muehlan and Katie Fortune (Kingwood, TX: Hunter Books, 1983), p. 102.

4. Curt Landry was part of many of these meetings and was witness to the hand of God in some of these events.

5. Lightle, *Exodus II,* p. 114.

6. Charles H. Spurgeon, *Metropolitan Tabernacle Pulpit* series of sermons, vol. 17, pp. 703-704, quoted in Iain H. Murray, *The Puritan Hope: Revival and the Interpretation of Prophecy* (1971; repr., Carlisle, PA: The Banner of Truth Trust, 1998), p. 256.

7. Quoted in William L. Hull, *The Fall and Rise of Israel* (Grand Rapids, MI: Zondervan Publishing House, 1954), p. 208. Emphasis added.

8. Ibid.

9. Theodor Herzl, quoted in Martin Gilbert, *Israel: A History* (New York: William Morrow and Company, 1998), p. 15.

10. James Hastings in *Dictionary of the Bible, Revised Edition* by Frederick C. Grant and H. H. Rowley (New York: Charles Scribner's Sons, 1963), p. 751.

JERUSALEM RESTORED
TO ISRAEL

*This is what the LORD Almighty says: "Once again men and
women of ripe old age will sit in the streets of Jerusalem, each with
cane in hand because of his age. The city streets will be
filled with boys and girls playing there."*

ZECHARIAH 8:4-5

In early 1967, Egypt ordered the United Nations' peacekeeping
troops out of the Sinai Peninsula, proceeded to blockade the
Strait of Tiran, cut off Israel's southern access to the Red Sea
and moved troops and artillery into the Sinai. In the north,
Syrian gunners, from their advantageous positions along the
Golan Heights, had continued to harass Jewish farmers and fishermen on the Sea of Galilee and were waiting eagerly for a
chance to demolish all Jewish settlements in that area.

In April of that year, on my first visit to Israel just weeks
before the Six-Day War, I had lunch at the *kibbutz* (a communal
settlement or farm) on the southern end of the Sea of Galilee.
Although I had not been a student of biblical prophecy and had
no sense that prophecy was being fulfilled by Israel's return to
the Land, I noticed the pockmarks on the buildings of the En
Gev Kibbutz Hotel, where I lunched; they were scars from the
Syrian guns that had shelled the kibbutz days earlier.

On this trip I learned that in Israel's 1948 War of Independence, Jordanian soldiers had destroyed the Jewish communities
in the Jewish Quarter of the Old City, had blown up synagogues
and houses, and had desecrated the Jewish cemeteries on the
Mount of Olives, but they had nonetheless been unsuccessful in
thwarting the establishment of the Jewish state. In June 1967,
these Jordanian troops, remembering the defeat of 19 years previous, waited to see what would happen in the south before they
began to attack Western Jerusalem. They soon received word
from Egyptian President Nasser that his invasion into the Sinai

was succeeding, although in fact the entire Egyptian air force had already been decimated and Israel was pushing Egypt all the way back across the Sinai Desert. Jordan trusted Nasser's word and immediately began marching west from East Jerusalem, intending to sweep decisively across the small nation of Israel. Syria was likewise encouraged to begin its descent into the Galilee from the Golan Heights.

But things did not progress as the Arab armies had imagined. Within six days, Israel's small, predominantly civilian army had pushed its enemies back on all fronts in one of the most astonishing military operations in history. Jerusalem was in the hands of a sovereign Israeli state for the first time since King Zedekiah had been taken to Babylon in 586 B.C. (unless one considers the short-lived Maccabean interval or the Bar Kokhba revolt).

The promise of God and the timing of God were again intersecting. Yet much of the Christian world was unaware of this, just as much of the Jewish world seemed to have ignored the unusual events surrounding the birth of Jesus 2,000 years earlier.

WHEN THE FIG TREE BLOOMS

Jesus predicted Jerusalem's history with great accuracy. He told His disciples that they should expect armies to surround the city of Jerusalem (see Luke 21:20). The city would be left desolate, and Jerusalem's citizens would be scattered into *all* the nations, which is what Jesus called "the times of the Gentiles" (v. 24). Yet Jerusalem would again be inhabited by the sons of Israel. Jesus even indicated the timing of their return—when the fig tree begins to blossom.

In prophetic literature, trees refer to the nations. The fig tree, in particular, has long been a prophetic symbol of the nation of Israel. "When I found Israel," declared God, speaking through Hosea, "it was like finding grapes in the desert; when I saw your fathers, it was like seeing the early fruit on the fig tree" (9:10).

Joel used this fig-tree imagery in his prophecy about the enemy forces that would soon devour the Land: "A nation has invaded my land, powerful and without number; it has the teeth of a lion, the fangs of a lioness. It has laid waste my vines and ruined my fig trees" (1:6-7).

Jesus' word to His disciples that day in Jerusalem was, therefore, a coded message: "Now learn this lesson from the fig tree: As soon as its twigs get tender and its leaves come out, you know that summer is near. Even so, when you see all these things, you know that it is near, right at the door" (Matt. 24:32-33; with parallel passages in Mark 13:28-29 and Luke 21:29-31).

What was Jesus' message? *When the nation of Israel is reborn, God's timing will have arrived*—but not before a series of historical events will have taken place first.

The Scattering

Jesus predicted the destruction that would come to the city: "When you see Jerusalem being surrounded by armies, you will know that its desolation is near. How dreadful it will be in those days . . . ! There will be great distress in the land and wrath against this people" (Luke 21:20,23).

The believing community in Jerusalem remembered Jesus' words a little over three decades later, in A.D. 66, when the Roman general Titus laid siege to the city. Within four years, the sacred Temple and the entire city were annihilated. Recalling that Jesus had said, "Let those who are living in Jerusalem flee" (see Luke 21:21), the believing community escaped across the Jordan to a place called Pella.

Three Exiles

By 721 B.C., the leading citizens of the northern kingdom of Israel had been taken to Assyria, from which many had been dispersed into the world. By 586 B.C., Babylon had invaded the southern kingdom of Judah, had destroyed the city of Jerusalem and the First Temple (erected under Solomon) and had carried to Babylon the king, nobles and leaders for a 70-year forced exile.

ISRAEL'S CONQUEST OF JERUSALEM IN 1967 WAS GOD'S EXCLAMATION POINT TO A WATCHING WORLD THAT THE PROPHETIC TIMETABLE WAS ON SCHEDULE.

The exile of which Jesus spoke, however, was not an exile to one nation, but to all the nations—an amazing prediction that has proven itself true even into this twenty-first century. Descendants of Israel still reside in North and South America, Europe, New Zealand and Australia, but also in various nations throughout Africa, as well as in Jewish settlements in China, India and Asia.

Until . . .

"Jerusalem will be trampled on by the Gentiles" (Luke 21:24), Jesus went on to say. From the time of the destruction of the Second Temple in A.D. 70 until modern times, no sovereign government of Israel had successfully reestablished the nation. Israeli rule happened only after the Jordanians were driven back in the Six-Day War of 1967. Only then did the words of Jesus find fulfillment.

"Jerusalem will be trampled on by the Gentiles until . . . ," Jesus said. The word "until" clearly speaks of a reversal of events—

a time when the Jewish people would regather in Jerusalem. Israel's conquest of Jerusalem in 1967 was God's exclamation point to a watching world that the prophetic timetable that had begun with the birth of the State of Israel was right on schedule.

THE TIMES OF THE GENTILES

"Jerusalem will be trampled on by the Gentiles, until the times of the Gentiles are fulfilled," Jesus continued (Luke 21:24). Prior to 1967, many prophecy teachers within the Church had assumed that Jesus' expression "the times of the Gentiles" implied that the Gentile part of the Church would be taken away in the rapture[1] before God turned His attention to the nation of Israel. This was the prevailing thought in much of the Church before the events of 1967. Martin and Johanna Chernoff expressed their own disappointment when, in the Hebrew Christian Alliance meetings following the June 1967 war, there was no mention of the return of Jerusalem to Israel, since the prophecy teachers had not had sufficient time to rearrange their belief system and redraw their charts.[2]

Paul obviously did not understand Jesus' words to imply that no more Gentiles would be saved after God began to deal with Israel, or else he would not have spoken of "greater riches" awaiting the nations when Israel returned (see Rom. 11:12; there will be more on this in chapter 5 of this book).

Then to what does "the times of the Gentiles" refer? Try to imagine what Jesus' disciples would have thought. It was no doubt inconceivable to them that faith in their long-awaited Messiah would be so completely embraced by Gentile believers that much of the Church, in our time, would all but have forgotten that the earliest believers were Jewish.

THE HISTORICAL PHASES
OF THE CHURCH

By mentioning the "times of the Gentiles," Jesus and later Rabbi Shaul (the apostle Paul) in his letter to the Romans (11:25) were, in fact, referring to one of the historical phases that would come in the life of the body of Messiah: (1) the totally Jewish church of the first decades; (2) the transition to Gentile dominance; (3) the centuries-long Gentile Church; (4) the present transition period in which both Jews and Gentiles are again a part of the church; and (5) the salvation of all of Israel and the return of the Jewish King as World Ruler, with his 12 apostles as "cabinet" members in the new administration (see Matt. 19:28). Let's take a look at some of the highlights of these five historical phases.

Phase One: The Early Jewish "Church"

The members of the Early Church, as described in Acts 1 through 9—composed of the 12 apostles, the 120 disciples who waited in the Upper Room, the 3,000 new believers on the following *Shavuot* (Pentecost) and the 5,000 who soon followed—were all Jewish, either naturally born or proselytes (see 1:15; 2:11,14,41; 4:4).

Even the Ethiopian eunuch was Jewish. This treasurer of Queen Candace of Ethiopia, returning from a time of worship in Jerusalem, was reading from the book of the Jewish prophet Isaiah when Philip found him in his chariot (see Acts 8:27-28). He may have been a part of the Jewish presence that had been in Ethiopia for several centuries or he may have been a convert to Judaism, but a Gentile believer he was not. That door remained closed until Peter's Joppa housetop experience and his subsequent visit with Cornelius (see Acts 10).

Phase Two: The Transitional Church
(From Jewish to Predominantly Gentile)

No apostle had ever preached the gospel to a non-Jew until Peter had his all-kinds-of-animals-and-reptiles vision at Simon the tanner's house in Joppa (see Acts 10:11-12). Without that vision, Peter would have been unwilling to go to the home of the Roman centurion Cornelius. That visit was the turning point in church history, an open door to the nations to receive the Jewish Messiah as Redeemer of all the nations, just as Isaiah had predicted: "Nations that do not know you will hasten to you" (55:5).

Even though Jesus had told His disciples that the gospel was to be taken to the nations (see Matt. 28:19-20; Acts 1:8), they would have assumed that Gentiles would also be required to submit to some changes in religious practice—that they would have to become *Torah*-observant (observe the books of the Law), for example. The Cornelius encounter proved otherwise when his uncircumcised household received an outpouring of the Holy Spirit equal to that given to the apostles at Pentecost (see Acts 11:15).

It seems that Peter and the six brothers who accompanied him to the house of Cornelius (see Acts 11:12) had a lot of explaining to do when "the apostles and the brothers throughout Judea heard that the Gentiles also had received the word of God. . . . The circumcised believers criticized him and said, 'You went into the house of uncircumcised men and ate with them'" (vv. 2-3). But after Peter and his companions told of all that had happened, the circumcised believers "had no further objections" (v. 18).

These objections were raised again later, however, and a special council had to be called in Jerusalem to decide how the Gentiles were to be received (see Acts 15). The apostles and leaders in Jerusalem spent many hours together before they finally came to an agreement. The Gentiles were in. They did not have to become Jewish proselytes, thus opening the door for rapid expansion of the Church among non-Jews. Although Paul, the apostle to the Gentiles, considered all believers to be a part of one body, he did make a distinction in the way in which Jews and non-Jews were accepted in the ministry. He insisted that Timothy, whose mother was Jewish (see Acts 16:1-3), should be circumcised, though he placed no such requirement on Titus, both of whose parents were Gentile (see Gal. 2:3).

As Paul and others began to have much success in their ministry among the Gentiles, many of the new believers, being Roman, held on to their predisposition against the Jews. The Church was soon ruled exclusively by Gentile Christians who opposed the Jewish people, even their own brothers in the faith, who, like Paul, were faithful adherents to the Torah. "Do not boast over [the Jewish] branches. Do not be arrogant," Paul admonished the Roman believers (Rom. 11:18,20). After all, the gospel was still "first for the Jew" (1:16). Paul continued with his admonitions to the Roman Gentile church: "Theirs [the Jewish people] is the adoption as sons; theirs the divine glory, the covenants, the receiving of the law, the temple worship and the promises. Theirs are the patriarchs . . . and the human ancestry of Christ" (9:4-5). He wanted them to remember that all these blessings had come to them through a Jew (Jesus) and through the Jews (they had kept faith in God alive through the centuries). Yet Paul's warnings went unheeded by most of the Church for the next 19 centuries.

Phase Three: The Gentile Church
The destruction of Jerusalem, the Bar Kokhba revolt of the early second century, the dispersion into the nations and the growing number of Gentiles who accepted Jesus as the Christ (Messiah)[3]

all combined to bring into existence a <u>Gentile Church that forsook her Jewish heritage.</u> The Church was dominated entirely by Gentiles. Yes, there have been Jewish believers in Jesus through the years—men like Alfred Edersheim, the great nineteenth-century expositor of Scripture, and the British statesman and Prime Minister Benjamin Disraeli—but there was no Jewish expression of faith in the Jewish Messiah. No Jewish bishop (although there were still some in existence) was invited to the A.D. 325 Nicean Council.

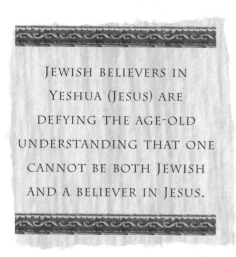

JEWISH BELIEVERS IN YESHUA (JESUS) ARE DEFYING THE AGE-OLD UNDERSTANDING THAT ONE CANNOT BE BOTH JEWISH AND A BELIEVER IN JESUS.

Soon after, Jewish believers were forced to leave all Jewish customs behind and to become part of the Gentile Church. The promises and blessings given to Abraham were then assumed to be the exclusive inheritance of the Church; the curses were all that remained for the Jews. This "replacement theology," though it began to be questioned in the sixteenth century and has been totally rejected by a few Bible scholars since,[4] has remained the dominant view of much of the Church into this twenty-first century. But more and more, the fallacy of this theology is being recognized in our day, aided immensely by the emergence of the resurrected community of Jewish believers and the revelation that is coming to the Church.

Phase Four: The Messianic Jewish Movement

We are presently experiencing another transition in which Jewish believers are back on the scene as a part of the larger body of believers in Yeshua (Jesus). Forty years ago there was not a single congregation established to foster the continuing Jewish identity of Jews who believe in Jesus. Today there are 400 or more congregations throughout the United States, the former Soviet Union, Latin America, Israel and other countries. These believers are defying the age-old understanding that one cannot be both Jewish and a believer in Jesus.

And these Jewish believers are no longer a covert group. They have been featured in front-page articles in Jewish newspapers and on national television. They are soldiers and officers in the Israeli army, businessmen, lawyers and bankers. We are in another time of transition when the original heirs of the kingdom are back and are beginning to impact the Church and the world.

Phase Five: The Return to Jewish Leadership

Some people would like us to believe that God is finished with Israel and that the kingdom has been transferred to the Gentile heirs, but Jesus was still speaking to His Jewish disciples about the future kingdom of Israel just days before His ascension. It was those 40 days of teaching on the kingdom that prompted the apostolic question, "Lord, are you at this time going to restore the kingdom to Israel?" (Acts 1:6). Jesus' answer implied that the question was valid, but that the timing was still hidden (see v. 7; there will be more on this in chapter 9).

But Jesus had not finished describing future events. He continued, "There will be signs in the sun, moon and stars. On the earth, nations will be in anguish and perplexity at the roaring and tossing of the sea. Men will faint from terror, apprehensive of what is coming on the world, for the heavenly bodies will be shaken" (Luke 21:25-26).

To no other generation would these words have the meaning they do in this day of rockets, satellites, manned space shuttles, moon walks and nuclear warheads. There have always been wars, but never before have all the nations of the world faced terrorism without boundaries. Even His words about men fainting from terror, translated in the *King James Version* of the Bible as "men's hearts failing them for fear," provide a strange reminder of the increase in heart attacks in modern culture.

"When these things begin to take place, stand up and lift up your heads, because your redemption is drawing near," Jesus said (Luke 21:28). "When you see these things happening, you know that the kingdom of God is near. I tell you the truth, this generation will certainly not pass away until all these things have happened" (vv. 31-32). Since the generation to which Jesus was speaking has long since left the scene, He must be speaking to our day—the generation that is seeing the fulfillment of Israel's return to the Land and specifically to her governmental reentry into Jerusalem.

Some people may have difficulty believing that we can know the general timing of the Lord's return, but He seemed to think differently. He compared our generation to Noah's day, when the people knew the season of the flood but not the day or the hour the rains would begin (see Matt. 24:37-39). Paul compared the closing generation to a pregnant woman who knows the month, but not the day or hour, of her child's birth. Then he was careful to note that the Lord will *not* come to believers like a thief in the night; they will expect Him (see 1 Thess. 5:3-4). Jesus affirmed this to John in His revelation (see Rev. 3:3).

Prophecy can often only be understood when it is fulfilled. Jesus' disciples could not have understood His words that day on the Mount of Olives overlooking the temple. *The Temple destroyed? Israel dispersed to the nations? The times of the Gentiles? A regathering? What could all this mean?* they must have wondered.

We have a different vantage point as we see His words being ful-filled. This causes us to "stand up and lift up [our] heads, for [our] redemption is drawing near" (Luke 21:28). It also causes us to look with astonishment as Israel's eyes begin to open to her Messiah.

Notes

1. The word "rapture" symbolizes an event that Paul described in his first let-ter to the Thessalonians: "For the Lord himself will come down from heaven, with a loud command, with the voice of the archangel and with the trumpet call of God, and the dead in Christ will rise first. After that, we who are still alive and are left will be caught up together with them in the clouds to meet the Lord in the air. And so we will be with the Lord for-ever" (4:16-17).

2. In speaking of the Hebrew Christian Alliance meeting that followed the June 1967 war, Yohanna Chernoff writes, "We had fully expected the con-ference leaders to tie the wonderful events of the Six-Day War and all their ramifications with prophecies from both Covenants. Incredibly, not one speaker preached on it; not one teacher taught on it; not one person said anything about it to us.

"Unaware that not even one, among the renowned theologians and prophetic scholars, had ever, even once, predicted that Jerusalem would be back in Jewish hands prior to the return of the Messiah at the very end of the Great Tribulation, we considered it to be a wonderful fulfill-ment of prophecy. All the scholars at that conference, however, played down the significance of Jerusalem returning to the Jews because it did not fit into their theology. Most of them were Scofield Dispensation-alists who believed, according to Luke 21:24, which says, *'Jerusalem shall be trodden down of the Gentiles, until the times of the Gentiles be fulfilled'* (KJV), that this could only occur after the Church was raptured out of the world and before the Great Tribulation Period. The fact that Jerusalem had already returned to Jewish rule meant to them that the 'Times of the Gentiles' had already ended, and that threw their theology into disar-ray." Yohanna Chernoff, *Born a Jew . . . Die a Jew: The Story of Martin*

Chernoff, A Pioneer in Messianic Judaism (Hagerstown, MD: Ebed Publications, 1996), pp. 103-104.

3. The name "Christ" is based on *Christos,* the Greek word that means the Anointed One. "Messiah" is based on *Mashiach,* the equivalent Hebrew term. James Strong, *The New Strong's Exhaustive Concordance of the Bible* (Nashville, TN: Thomas Nelson Publishers, 1984), Hebrew ref. no. 4899 and Greek ref. no. 5547.

4. See appendix B.

CHAPTER 4

THE OPENING OF
JEWISH EYES

Then their eyes were opened and they recognized him.

LUKE 24:31

On my trip to Israel in the fall of 2004, I was ushered aside at a passport checkpoint, where I waited for several minutes before being summoned into an adjoining room. I sat across the table from my two interrogators.

Their first question had to do with an illegal political organization that they thought I might know something about. When I assured them that I had never heard of the organization, one of the agents asked, "Why do you come to Israel so often?"[1]

"I am a Christian pastor and have brought many groups to Israel through the years," I replied. "This time I will be speaking at the International Christian Embassy Jerusalem's Feast of Tabernacles celebration next week."[2] Then I dared to mention, "Actually, I am also very involved worldwide with Jewish people who believe that Yeshua is the Messiah."

"Oh, you are!" they smiled broadly, knowing that I had ventured into an often forbidden territory. In earlier years I would have tried to avoid that subject.

Encouraged by their response, I added, "I know it's controversial, but it is not illegal."

They grinned, we exchanged a few more remarks, and then they waved me off to rejoin my group. "Enjoy your time in Israel. Sorry for the inconvenience."

TURNING POINT

When I began making frequent trips to Israel, I was hesitant to speak of Jewish people who believe in Jesus, lest I expose them to further scrutiny or persecution. As a result, I did not always know how to respond to the airport inquiries about those I would be visiting.

That all changed in June 2000 when I was checking in with El Al Airlines in New York. I had been to this counter many times previously, so I knew of their meticulous questioning before boarding the aircraft.

"I have receipts for everything I brought with me," I volunteered, as my young agent began her inspection. "I have been to Israel many times, have friends in the Land, and am aware that everything I pack has to be well-documented."

My unsmiling gate agent responded with a barrage of questions: "What kinds of things do you have? Why are you bringing so much? Who are your friends in the Land?"

"I have friends all over the Land," I replied, trying to be a little evasive.

She would not easily relent. "Who, for example?"

I pondered for only a moment. *OK, I'll just go for it. After all, it is not as though my believing-in-Yeshua friends in the Land are hiding.* Messianic Jews are well known by the Ministry of Interior and certainly by the *Yad L'Achim,* a group of ultra-Orthodox Jewish leaders who are unequivocally opposed to and who actively persecute Israeli Jewish believers in Jesus.

"I realize that this is a bit controversial," I began, "but I work with and support Jewish people who believe that Yeshua is the Messiah."

"You do?" She paused in her examination of my luggage and stared at me, her eyes widening. "Are there very many?"

"Perhaps several hundred thousand."

"Really? Do any of them live in Israel?"

"Approximately 6,000 or 7,000, I would say."

"Well, that seems to be a lot for such a small country. Do they all live together?"

"Oh, no, they live all over the Land. They are in business, in the army, everywhere . . . in fact, I have written a book about it," I added a bit reluctantly.

She seemed interested. "Did you bring a copy with you?" she inquired.

"No, but I do have the manuscript."[3]

"Could I see it?"

"Of course," I said, as I pulled out the bound sheaf of papers and began to read through the table of contents with her:

Chapter 1
The Beginning of the End

Not until I was challenged to take another look at the Scriptures—the prophets, the apostles and Jesus Himself—did I become aware that God still has a plan for His covenant people and that their return to their ancestral home signals the beginning of the end.

Chapter 2
The "Greater Riches" World Revival

The unparalleled growth of the Church in our day, heralding the greatest awakening in world history, is connected to the rebirth of Israel.

Chapter 3
Israel—A Nation of Priests

Israel and the Jewish people have made a profound impact—both secular and spiritual—on the nations and have kept alive faith in the one true God.

I glanced up. The young gate agent was still with me, so I read on.

Chapter 4
The Targeted Annihilation
*From the call of Abraham down to the present time,
man's invisible enemy has targeted Israel for extinction
in order to thwart the purposes of God and abort His
promises.*

Chapter 5
The Early Jewish "Church"
*Although salvation was accomplished through the com-
pleted work of the Messiah alone, the all-Jewish Early
Church continued to observe Sabbath and celebrate the
feasts as a proclamation of the Messiah who had fulfilled them.*

Chapter 6
The "Gentilizing" of the Church
*When the Romans destroyed the Temple and the city of
Jerusalem, the Church assumed that God was finished
with Israel and soon demanded that Jewish believers
forsake their own heritage.*[4]

I continued to read, but my interrogator was looking uneasy
and seemed no longer to be listening. As I paused, she began the
final questioning: "Did you pack your own luggage? Have your
bags been in your possession the entire time? Has anyone given
you anything to take with you?"

I had been standing at the ticket counter only a short time,
but she was already attaching the required clearance stamps for
me to board. When she finished with the stamps, she asked that
my traveling companion and I step aside for a few minutes while
they completed our boarding procedure.

Michael, my traveling companion on this trip, and I sat down, wondering what had just happened. I had brought up a subject that had always been better left untouched. Jewish believers in Jesus are sometimes refused citizenship in Israel, as though they are no longer Jews. Would the Passport Control Office now forbid our entrance into Israel?

After what seemed an interminably long wait, our gate agent came over to us, bringing our boarding passes, tickets and passports, and then made a rather astonishing statement: "Thank you for what you are doing. It is very important."

We walked to the gate, puzzled. Had we just met a fellow believer? Did this woman know some Messianic Jews, whom she considered to be loyal citizens? Was she a secular Jew who disliked the way the Yad L'Achim often tries to dictate the faith of the country? Did she recognize with gratitude our love for the Jewish people? Why was our mission important to her, as she had stated it to be? Whatever the reason, the incident forever changed the way I would relate to government agencies in Israel about the Messianic Jewish movement in the future.

RAPHAEL

Believers in Jesus are no longer a frightened community in hiding—no longer a strange phenomenon either in Israel or in other nations.

One of my newer acquaintances in the Land, Raphael,[5] made aliyah when his children were quite young and now leads a Messianic fellowship of believers. Because of this association, he was once summoned to appear before the Ministry of the Interior.

A lawyer friend of his, also a believer, wrote a letter to the Ministry of the Interior, asking about the nature of the inquiry. Some weeks later, the legal counsel was informed that the matter had to do with Raphael's citizenship. The lawyer responded that his client's citizenship was not in question, that Raphael and his family had been loyal Israeli citizens for many years, that their children had served and continue to serve in the Israeli army and that such a summons was, therefore, unconstitutional.

They never heard back from the government office. The first letter was obviously an attempt to intimidate, probably by some lesser official who was spurred into action by the more orthodox sectors who would like to see all Jewish believers in Jesus expelled from the Land. In the ensuing months, there were articles in the Israeli newspapers, discussions on national television stations and other public mention of the gradually increasing Messianic Jewish population of Israel as simply another anomaly in the history of this unusual nation, whose citizens have returned from their "exile" to over 100 foreign nations.

RIVKA

Rivka was reared on a secular kibbutz. As a young adult, she found this lifestyle to be unfulfilling, and she moved to Jerusalem to study under a rabbi and become Orthodox. A series of God-encounters changed all that, and instead, she became an ardent disciple of Yeshua, the Jewish Messiah. A few years later, her Messianic congregation suggested that she give her testimony at an assembly to which she would invite all of her former kibbutz friends as special guests. When the Yad L'Achim found out about Rivka's invitation, they wrote letters to her former colleagues at the kibbutz, warning them that she had, in their view, become a traitor to her faith. Her friends on the kibbutz were so incensed by the religious community's attempt to tell them what to do that they turned out in force to hear the testimony.

On the night of the gathering, the Yad L'Achim stationed representatives outside the gathering place to try to discourage anyone from entering the building. When Rivka's congregational leader realized what was happening, he stepped outside and motioned to the religious vigilantes to come nearer. "We want to thank you," he said as they approached. "We probably would not have had nearly the turnout if you had not helped us publicize this event!"

THE MESSIANIC MOVEMENT, BOTH INSIDE AND OUTSIDE OF ISRAEL, IS A FORCE THAT CAN NO LONGER BE DENIED.

This is a new day in Israel. Yes, there is still harassment of many believers in Jesus. There are times when assembly halls are not rented to Messianic congregations because the landlords fear the rabbis who threaten boycotts of various sorts, but this is gradually changing. The Messianic movement, both inside and outside of Israel, is a force that can no longer be denied.

STEVE, ARLENE, RACHEL AND OTHERS

Steve was president of his Conservative synagogue when he accepted an invitation to attend a service in a small storefront congregation of Messianic Jewish believers, and immediately knew that he was home. Arlene was attending a friend's wedding at a church when she felt strangely drawn to the people and their message. Dominique was launched into a quest for more knowledge about the Jewish rabbi Jesus after being expelled from her *yeshiva* (a school providing religious instruction) for asking about this forbidden Teacher. Rachel was in her Orthodox Jewish home, crying out for more of God, when she heard a voice say, *Get in touch with the Messianic Jews.* Frann was in her car, considering seeing a psychiatrist, when she heard, *Come to Me!* Curt, who had been resisting the One who had captured the heart of his wife, was overcome with the power of God while in his Jacuzzi. Amnon was sunburned from the Light that filled his hotel room during a time of seeking after God. Jacques was in an American jail, detained for working without a green card, when he felt the Presence enter his cell. Rene felt waves of fire and love flowing over him when he stepped into an historic church away from his Israeli homeland; soon after, he learned about his Jewish Messiah and is now passionately introducing Him to others.

What do all these people have in common?

They are Jewish men and women who have come to faith or are inquiring about Jesus as Messiah in this unique generation—the first time this has happened in such large numbers since the first centuries of the Common Era. They began to come during the Jesus Movement of the late 1960s and early 1970s. They found their way during and following the collapse of Soviet communism. Jewish communities in Latin America and other nations began to be affected. This change has even touched lives of the *sabra* (native Israelis) inside Israel. Soon every facet of life in the Land was infiltrated with believers. The existence of these believers, who have not ceased to be Jewish, can no longer be ignored. They often do not identify with the word "Christian," a designation that has its origin in the Greek "Christos" (Christ) rather than in the Hebrew "Maschiach" (Messiah). Nor are they always estranged from the larger Jewish community.

In one city in South America, the Messianic congregation enjoys a good relationship with most of the traditional Jewish community; the congregations are mutually supportive, and Messianic believers are even allowed use of the facilities in the local Jewish community center. Some Orthodox Jews are now enrolled in the correspondence courses sponsored by the Messianic community.[6] Sid Roth was ministering in Siberia when he met an Orthodox rabbi who expressed a desire to believe in Jesus. Following their conversation, the rabbi invited Sid to come and teach his congregation of 200 people.[7] In Belarus, the relationship of Messianic Jews and their traditional brothers and sisters is reminiscent of the days of the Early Church, when both Jews and Gentiles inquired together about Jesus.[8]

For as long as I have been traveling to Israel, the King of Kings congregation has held services in the Jerusalem YMCA across from the King David Hotel on King David Street. Wayne and Ann Hilsden have been faithful to their call of ministering to the English-speaking expatriate community and to Israeli believers. In addition to helping to plant two other Hebrew-speaking congregations in the 1980s and 1990s, they have begun another Hebrew-speaking congregation that reaches out to the native Israelis as well as to those returning from the nations.

The impact of this congregation is now changing. With the help of the international community of believers and the extraordinary vision of Wayne, Ann and their leaders, the King of Kings congregation has opened the "Pavilion" in what was once the largest theater in downtown Jerusalem, at the corner of Jaffa Road and Prophet Street. The new assembly hall will be used for concerts and drama productions as well as for congregational meetings. Attitudes are shifting—even in downtown Jerusalem.

PROPHECY FULFILLED IN OUR DAY

Isaiah knew that this time would come. These are the people of whom the Lord was speaking when He told the prophet that there would be a time of closed eyes and ears and of hardened hearts.

But this time will be reversed. Eyes will be opened again—when the cities no longer lay "ruined and without inhabitant" (6:11). Ears will hear again—when the houses are no longer "deserted and the fields ruined and ravaged" (v. 11). Hearts will soften again—when the Land is no longer "utterly forsaken" (v. 12). Israel's response to God will occur when she, "the holy seed," returns to the Land and when she, "the stump," begins to grow again (v. 13). This is that day!

Hosea also knew about our day. "Afterward the Israelites . . . will come trembling to the LORD and to his blessings in the last days," the prophet assured all future generations (3:5). This would happen after many years without a king and without a sacrifice. Israel's last king was sent into exile in the sixth century before Jesus, and her sacrifices ceased when the Second Temple was destroyed by Rome in A.D. 70. Our day is the "afterward" to which Hosea referred.

THE SINGLE MOST IMPORTANT FULFILLMENT OF BIBLE PROPHECY IN THE LAST 2,000 YEARS IS THE RETURN OF ISRAEL TO HER LAND OF INHERITANCE.

Ezekiel was also not ignorant of the significance of our time. Not only did he see the resurrection of the nation of Israel in his dry-bones vision, but he also saw this season as a time when Israel would come to know her God and would be filled with His Spirit. Ezekiel knew that this awakening would occur at a time when Israel was surrounded by enemies who were claiming her land as their own possession. "Aha! The ancient heights have become our possession," they would say (36:2). And this is what is happening!

Israel's return is to be a time of reinhabiting the towns and rebuilding the ruins. With words similar to those of Isaiah (see 6:11-13), Ezekiel prophesied, "I will multiply the number of people upon you. . . . The towns will be inhabited and the ruins rebuilt. . . . I will settle people on you as in the past and will make you prosper more than before. *Then you will know that I am the* LORD*"* (36:10-11; emphasis added). *Then* you will know! When? *When* you return!

Ezekiel even saw that Israel would be brought back in unbelief:

> It is not for your sake, O house of Israel, that I am going to do these things, but for the sake of my holy name, which you have profaned among the nations where you have gone. I will give you a new heart and put a new spirit in you; I will remove from you your heart of stone [another Isaiah-like reference to a calloused heart; see Isa. 6:10] and give you a heart of flesh. And I will put my Spirit in you and move you to follow my decrees and be careful to keep my laws (36:22,26-27).

Why did Raphael, Rivka, Steve, Arlene, Dominique, Rachel, Frann, Curt, Amnon, Jacques, Rene and a host of others experience this supernatural calling of God? Because the time of which Isaiah, Hosea and Ezekiel spoke is upon us. God's promise has intersected with His timing, and many Jewish people are receiving supernatural revelation of their God.

ALL ISRAEL WILL BE SAVED!

Our first-century Jewish brother Paul was also aware of a future time when Israel would receive the Messiah. There would be a hardening of hearts *until,* he says, a significant number of

Gentiles had entered the kingdom; then *"all Israel will be saved"* (Rom. 11:26, emphasis added).

This hardening of hearts, Gentile dominance and the return of Israel to the kingdom were the subjects of much of Jesus' teaching, but His disciples could not comprehend what He was saying. "You will not see me again," He told the Jewish leaders, "until you say, 'Blessed is he who comes in the name of the Lord' " (Matt. 23:39). This statement obviously implies that He would return, but also that Israel's leaders would one day receive Him as Messiah.

The single most important fulfillment of Bible prophecy in the last 2,000 years is the return of Israel to her Land of Inheritance. This was soon followed by the fulfillment of Jesus' words shortly before His death, when He spoke specifically of the Jewish return to the city of Jerusalem. The resurrection of the Jewish believing community is likewise a coming together of God's promises with His timing in our day.

A BLESSING TO THE NATIONS

The Jewish people are not the only people affected by their return to their ancient homeland. Israel was chosen for God's blessings to flow both into the family of Abraham, Isaac and Jacob, and into the nations. The "chosen ones"[9] have been and will yet become a light to the rest of the world. "I will take hold of your hand," God spoke through Isaiah, "I will keep you and will make you to be a covenant for the people and a light for the Gentiles" (42:6).

Notes

1. Since 1997, I have made two or three trips a year to Israel to encourage Messianic leaders, to speak at conferences, to introduce other leaders to the Land and to its people, or to take prayer and ministry groups to the Land.

2. The International Christian Embassy Jerusalem has enjoyed great governmental favor in Israel during its 25 year existence. The Christian Embassy was established as a way of letting the world know that many Christians stand with Israel's claim to the Land, even though their governments may not have acknowledged Jerusalem as Israel's capital. Israel is the only nation of the world that is not allowed to name its own capital—in spite of the fact that King David made this city the capital of the nation 3,000 years ago when he defeated the Jebusites. Even though the United States Congress voted to move the American Embassy to Jerusalem from Tel Aviv and even though both President Bill Clinton and President George W. Bush agreed with this vote, the Embassy has yet to be relocated.

3. This event took place in 2000, the year before *Your People Shall Be My People* was published.

4. Don Finto, *Your People Shall Be My People* (Ventura, CA: Regal Books, 2001).

5. Some of the names in this book have been changed to protect individual privacy.

6. Marcelo Miranda Guimaraes, "Restoration in Brazil," *Messianic Jewish Bible Institute Update*, Fall 2004.

7. Sid Roth, "Dear Mishpochah," *Messianic Vision Newsletter*, September 2004, p. 3 and November 2004, n.p.

8. From an update of the Shalom Network International (P.O. Box 72; Webster, New York 14580), Fall 2004.

9. The Bible uses the name "chosen ones" to refer to the Jewish people. See 1 Chronicles 16:13 and Psalm 105:6,43 for some examples.

REVIVAL AMONG THE NATIONS

Look at the nations and watch—and be utterly amazed.
For I am going to do something in your days that you would
not believe, even if you were told.

HABAKKUK 1:5

"You will be my witnesses . . . to the ends of the earth," Jesus reminded His disciples that day on the Mount of Olives shortly before His ascent into heaven (Acts 1:8). And He could have added, "I will not be back until this gospel of the Kingdom has reached every *ethnos* [people groups within a nation][1] of the world" (see Matt. 24:14). The apostle Paul was the most effective "missionary"[2] in the first century, reaching the ends of the Roman world with the message that Messiah had come.

In the intervening years since the first century, though the message of Jesus has had tremendous impact on the Western world and Western civilization, it has had much less influence on the continents of Africa and Asia. But as of the last century, a Christian tsunami has washed over virgin territory and is rapidly changing the world's spiritual landscape.

None of this would have taken the apostle Paul or the prophet Ezekiel by surprise. In Paul's letter to the Romans, he foresaw a time when the Jewish people who, as a nation, had rejected their Messiah, would come to faith. When that happens and they come into their fullness (see Rom. 11:12), there will be a time of "greater riches" for the whole world (see 11:15). Five centuries before Jesus came, Ezekiel not only predicted the resurrection of the nation of Israel from the dead (see Ezek. 37:1-11), but also that the world would come to know the Lord when He showed Himself powerful through the nation of Israel (see 37:23).

Philip Jenkins, Distinguished Professor of History and Religious Studies at Penn State University, has written an eye-opening book called *The Next Christendom*. Jenkins submits not only that one out of every three of the world's citizens now calls himself or herself Christian but also that the strength of the Church has shifted from the West to the East and to the South.[3] World missions statisticians tell us that China, Latin America and Africa are all reporting 25,000 to 30,000 new believers a day. China had fewer than 1 million believers in 1949, when communism overtook the country; today, China is home to as many as 120 million believers.[4] Strong revival pockets dot the landscape of other Asian nations and of Latin America. The continent of Africa was only about 8 to 9 percent Christian at the turn of the twentieth century; it had risen to over 45 percent at the beginning of the twenty-first century.[5]

THE GROWING CHURCH OF AFRICA

In a meeting held in 2002, 30 miles from Lagos, Nigeria's largest city, more than 2 million people, perhaps as many as 4 million, from over 2 dozen African nations attended a 3-day Christian festival. Five thousand security guards were posted on the 4,000-acre tract of land used for the gathering. Plastic garbage bags—for the collection of offerings—were passed through the crowd by 10,000 ushers positioned in every sector of the assembly. A 40-man crew spent three weeks laying 1 million meters of cable so that all could hear the music and preaching. Buses were used to bring new converts to the front for prayers and counseling.[6]

In 2004, Peter Wagner visited Nigeria and attended an all-night prayer meeting of the Redeemed Christian Church of God, where he found half a million people praying through the night. At that time, the building—the size of 69 football fields—was still being enlarged.[7]

The Church in Nigeria has recognized her call to be a witness for the Lord. The Redeemed Christian Church of God, by 2004, had spawned over 6,000 affiliate churches in more than 50 nations, including 150 in the United States.[8]

Faith Tabernacle, a congregation that meets in its 50,400-seat worship center at Canaan Land, Ota, Nigeria, is pastored by David Oyedepo. Bishop Oyedepo is the president of Covenant University, designed to train 6,500 students from every African nation, and the chairman of World Mission Agency, a missionary organization that, as of 2004, had branches in 30 African nations where 100,000 people had been equipped for effective leadership.[9]

One of the largest churches in Europe was planted by a Nigerian pastor. The Embassy of God Church in Kiev, Ukraine, is led by Pastor Sunday Adelaja. Started in 1994, just 10 years later, this church has over 20,000 members in its home congregation and has been used to begin 200 congregations in other countries, including the United Arab Emirates, the United States, Russia and the Netherlands.[10]

As of 2005, Nigeria was home to approximately 128 million, almost 50 percent of whom were professed Christians.[11] Most of this growth has come in the last century, with astonishing rapidity in the last decades.

The growth of the Church in Africa is not limited to Nigeria. During one eight-month period, 28 Ethiopian evangelists led 681 people to Jesus and started 683 house churches. The Maasai tribe in Kenya has been very resistant to the gospel; but in more recent years, five trained, lay Maasai evangelists began speaking to their families and tribes. These humble beginnings produced an additional 70 lay evangelists, who subsequently moved across Maasai territory, teaching and preaching and leading 15 percent of the 600,000 Maasai in Kenya to faith in Jesus.[12]

The number of professing Christians on the African continent has grown from 9 million to over 360 million during the past century.[13] And now, 1,200 new house churches are born each month in Africa.[14] This kind of church growth is all but unknown in the West.

THE ASTONISHING CHURCH OF CHINA

The growth of the Church in China has caught the attention of the entire Western world in the past few years. Numerous missions groups and churches have taken an interest in this often-persecuted body of believers. Some of us have been privileged to be a part of teams that carried in Bibles for the growing house-church movement. I still remember waiting in line in 1989 at the checkpoint out of Hong Kong, our suitcases, coat pockets and socks all stuffed with Bibles. Then, once inside China, we waited for nine hours at the airport

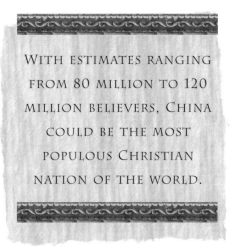

WITH ESTIMATES RANGING FROM 80 MILLION TO 120 MILLION BELIEVERS, CHINA COULD BE THE MOST POPULOUS CHRISTIAN NATION OF THE WORLD.

before we could board the plane to Beijing. By the time we arrived in Beijing, almost everyone at the airport had gone home. That long delay was one of God's ways of closing the Beijing Airport before our arrival so that not a piece of our luggage, which was loaded with Bibles, was checked. The next morning we carried all of our materials over to Sister Mabel's tiny apartment and saw her bookshelves filled with Bibles to be distributed to pastors and leaders who would be coming for the "bread."

Sister Mabel could not think of any way to thank us, so she took the Chinese calendar from her wall and gave it to us in gratitude. I still have one of the pages of that calendar and a picture of Sister Mabel adorning a wall in my office. "What can they do to me?" she said, as we inquired if she did not fear arrest for distributing Bibles. "I'm an old woman. I've been in prison before. They can kill me. I'll just meet the Lord that much quicker." I found out just recently that Sister Mabel lived another 15 years.

There is really no way to describe the Chinese Church. In some cities, government-approved churches are thriving with millions of registered Christians, but the real growth is "underground" in the house church movement. Bibles are printed in China and can be bought through the government-recognized churches, but there have also been stories of people who were followed as they left the approved church to go to a house church, only to face arrest when they arrived. Most of the Christians in the house church movements are still without Bibles. Many of the pastors do not even own one. A visiting foreigner, finding it odd that a house church met on Thursday afternoon, learned that this was the one time in the week when the congregation was allowed use of the only Bible in the area.

Chinese believer Brother Yun tells the story of his own conversion.[15] His mother had been a believer back before the Cultural Revolution, which took place in the 1960s and 1970s. But because church leaders were jailed or killed and church buildings burned, leaving no one to encourage Yun's mother, her faith had grown dormant. Years later, when Yun's father was at the point of death, Yun's mother heard a voice in the middle of the night that called, "Jesus loves you." She was so stirred by the memory and revelation that she arose from her bed, awakened her children and told them about Jesus. The whole family laid hands on the father, and he was restored to health.

Yun's mother, though she was illiterate and had not even seen a Bible, became the pastor of a growing church. It was many months later before Yun received his first Bible. It was brought to him in the night after 100 days of fasting, with only one bowl of rice daily. So grateful was Yun for his Bible that he first read it voraciously and then began to memorize a chapter a day. Six weeks later, he was asked to bring his first sermon; not knowing how to preach, he simply quoted all of Matthew and half of Acts!

Yun became one of the leaders in the underground Church in China. He was often beaten and imprisoned until, through a miraculous, Peter-type delivery (see Acts 12:5-11), he walked out of prison, on legs that had been brutally broken but restored, to a waiting taxi. The taxi took him to friends who assisted him in escaping the country. Today he lives in Germany and travels extensively to other countries to speak in behalf of the persecuted Church of China. I heard him when he appeared as the featured speaker at the 2004 International Christian Embassy Jerusalem's annual Feast of Tabernacles celebration.

Another Chinese Christian, Brother Danyun, traveled for six months on bicycle through some of the spiritual hot spots of China, collecting stories of the revival there. The experiences of our brothers and sisters are recorded in his book, *Lilies Amongst Thorns.* One story tells of a widowed mother of three, whose husband had been killed for his faith. When she, too, was arrested, her children were left in the care of church members. During the eight years of her incarceration, she was repeatedly threatened and brutally tortured, but she also experienced the supernatural presence of God and saw over half of the 1,500 fellow inmates and many of the guards come to faith. On the day of her release, she was so overwhelmed with emotion at the thought of leaving her flock that she stopped outside the prison walls and wept for a while before she could gain enough composure to reunite with her children and fellow Christians on the outside.[16]

No one knows the size of the Chinese Church. Estimates range from 80 million believers to as many as 120 million. China could be the most populous Christian nation of the world. Certainly it is one of the strongest.

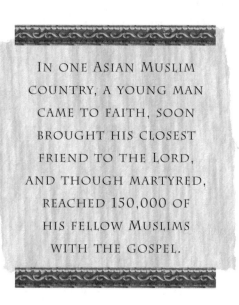

IN ONE ASIAN MUSLIM COUNTRY, A YOUNG MAN CAME TO FAITH, SOON BROUGHT HIS CLOSEST FRIEND TO THE LORD, AND THOUGH MARTYRED, REACHED 150,000 OF HIS FELLOW MUSLIMS WITH THE GOSPEL.

"China is in the process of becoming Christianized," writes David Aikman, former *Time* magazine Chief of Bureau in Beijing. "At the present rate of growth in the number of Christians in the country-side, in the cities, and especially within China's social and cultural establishment, it is possible that Christians will constitute 20 to 30 percent of China's population within three decades. If that should happen, it is almost certain that a Christian view of the world will be the dominant worldview within China's political and cultural establishment, and possibly within senior military circles."[17]

Aikman also reports what one of China's top research scholars said to him at their hotel one night in 2002. This Chinese scholar had come to some very surprising conclusions about the strength of America. "In the past twenty years, we have realized that the heart of your culture is your religion: Christianity. That is why the West has been so powerful. The Christian moral foundation of social and cultural life was what made possible the emergence of capitalism and then the successful transition to democratic politics. We don't have any doubt about this."[18]

In spite of such favorable comments by some of the Chinese elite, the growth of the Church has come with intense persecution. According to The Committee for Investigation on Persecution of Religion on China, Inc., in one small portion of the house-church movement, "23,686 house-church Christians have been arrested for religious activities, 4,014 sentenced to re-education, 129 killed, 208 handicapped, 997 placed under surveillance, 1,400 on the run, over 20,000 beaten, and 10,000 fined."[19] In June 2004, our sister Jiang Zongxiu was beaten to death by communist officials in China after she was arrested for passing out Bibles.[20]

THE EXPANSION INTO ASIA

Not only in China but also in other countries of Asia, the Church is growing in ways that have not been seen in the 20 centuries of its existence. The underground Church in North Korea is believed to have grown tenfold to a membership of 200,000 in the past decade.[21] The first church in Korea was planted in 1884;[22] now there are over 60,000 churches.[23] In 1900, Korea's population was less than 1 percent Christian;[24] today the number of Christians in South Korea is over 40 percent.[25] Some of the world's largest churches are in Seoul, the very largest numbering over 700,000.[26] South Korea is second only to the United States in sending missionaries for the purpose of world evangelism.[27]

South Vietnam had only 160,000 evangelical believers when the country fell to communism in 1975, but today there are an estimated 1 million. Most of the growth has occurred among the minority tribal groups of the Central Highlands and the Northwest provinces. Fifteen years ago, there were no Christians among the Hmong minority. Today there are reported to be

300,000 believers among a total of approximately 693,000 people. Another minority, the Ede, have seen their Christian numbers swell from 15,000 to 150,000 during the last 25 years.[28]

Exponential growth of the Church continues all throughout Asia. Indonesia, though the largest Muslim nation of the world, now has a Christian population of somewhere between 16 and 20 percent. And in Nepal, where no Christians were allowed in before 1960, the first church was begun in 1958 with 29 Christians; today there are over 500,000 in over 3,000 churches. Church-planting movements in Outer Mongolia and Inner Mongolia have produced more than 60,000 new Christians, while Cambodia's killing fields have come alive with more than 60,000 Christians. In one Southeast Asian country, during an eight-year period, almost a half million people came to faith. This number seemed so incredible that a team of researchers went to this country to be sure that the numbers were being reported accurately. The team found that the number could even be higher than had been reported![29]

THE MUSLIM AWAKENING

For centuries Christians had assumed that it was too difficult to lead Muslims to believe in Jesus. Yet that perception has been changing in the last decades. More Muslims have come to faith in the past two decades than in all the centuries preceding.

In one North African area, 16,000 Berbers turned to Jesus during a 20-year period. In Central Asia, 13,000 Kazakhs came to Him during a 15-year period. In South Asia, 12,000 Kashmiri Muslims have become believers as well.[30] In a certain Asian Muslim country, one young man came to faith and soon brought his closest friend into his new family. Though both were martyred for their faith, over the next 10 years, 150,000 of their fellow Muslims were reached with the gospel.[31]

Many of the new disciples from Muslim regions of the world have never seen a church building and have never known a paid evangelist, pastor or worker. Their house churches number from only a very few to as many as 50 or 60. Because they meet in Muslim nations, their gatherings are often on Friday, the only day free from work in the Muslim world.[32]

EZEKIEL, PAUL AND OUR DAY

This outbreak of revival around the world must have been what Ezekiel saw when he referred to a time in which the world would know the Lord because of His relationship to the regathered Israel (see Ezek. 36:23). This astonishing growth in the Body of Messiah is also no doubt that to which Paul was pointing when he spoke of the "greater riches" and "life from the dead" that would accompany Israel's "fullness" and "acceptance" (Rom. 11:12,15). This was the apostle's way of saying, "If you think the first coming of the Messiah has been good for the nations, just wait until *Israel* accepts Him! The whole world will be awakened to new life."

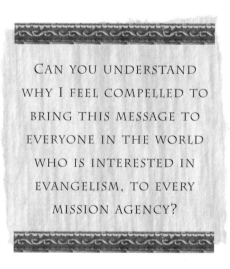

CAN YOU UNDERSTAND WHY I FEEL COMPELLED TO BRING THIS MESSAGE TO EVERYONE IN THE WORLD WHO IS INTERESTED IN EVANGELISM, TO EVERY MISSION AGENCY?

Through the centuries, most of the Church has not understood Paul's words, but around 450 years ago, a handful of scholars took another look. In the comments on Romans 11 in the

Geneva Bible of 1560, scholars spoke of the world being restored to new life when the Jewish people awaken to faith. Robert Leighton, Samuel Rutherford and many other scholars from earlier centuries saw the connection between the return of Israel to their Land and to the Lord and the revival that would reach around the world (see appendix B).

In 1716 Thomas Boston preached a sermon entitled "Encouragement to Pray for the Conversion of the Jews." He said, "Are you longing for a revival to the churches, now lying like dry bones, would you fain have the Spirit of life enter into them? Then pray for the Jews. For if the casting away of them be the reconciling of the world; what shall the receiving of them be, but life from the dead? . . . That will be a lively time, a time of a great outpouring of the Spirit, that will carry reformation to a greater height than yet has been."[33]

These amazing advances in evangelism are accompanied by an equally amazing increase in signs and wonders. James Rutz has researched this rather carefully in his book *Megashift*, in which he chronicles many of these miracles. In one instance, a woman was raised up from her sickbed of 21 years as the Gospel of Mark was read to her, after which 600 people in her village came to the Lord. In a four-year span, this number had increased to 70,000.[34] Rutz also recounts stories of a leper who was healed in a marketplace, of the gospel being preached in one language but understood in another, of a demonized man chained for years who was set free, of Jesus appearing in visions, and of many resurrections from the dead.[35] One such resurrection is partially recorded on video, in which a man, dead for almost two days, began to be restored at a Reinhold Bonnke meeting in Africa.[36]

Can you understand why I feel compelled to bring this message to everyone in the world who is interested in evangelism, to every mission agency? Do you see why the words of Ezekiel and

Paul pulsate through my spirit? If I am called to Mozambique or Afghanistan or Peru or Thailand, and understand that my salvation and theirs has come through the Jews—actually through *a* Jew—and that the Jewish return and world evangelism are connected, and if I give priority in my love and prayers to my Jewish brothers and sisters, whether or not they have yet come to faith, then I will have more faith for Mozambique, Afghanistan, Peru, Thailand or whatever country burns in my heart.

I agree with Jonathan Edwards that the coming of Israel to faith "will be before the glory of the Gentile part of the church shall be fully accomplished, because it is said that their coming in shall be life from the dead to the Gentiles" (see Rom. 11:12,15).[37] I want to be like Rees Howells, who spent many hours praying with his students when, in 1947, they saw the possibility that the nation of Israel would be reestablished.[38] I want to stand in the conviction of Charles Spurgeon, who believed that we do not attach enough importance to the restoration of Israel, that the fullness of the Church's glory can never come until the Jewish people acknowledge their Messiah. Spurgeon declared, "Matchless benefits to the world are bound up with the restoration of Israel; their gathering shall be as life from the dead."[39]

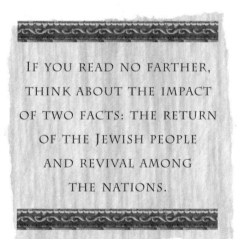

IF YOU READ NO FARTHER, THINK ABOUT THE IMPACT OF TWO FACTS: THE RETURN OF THE JEWISH PEOPLE AND REVIVAL AMONG THE NATIONS.

If you happen to be one of those people who begin reading a lot of books, but seldom finish one, let me encourage you to stop just now and ponder what you have read. If you read no farther, think about the impact of two facts: the return of the Jewish people and revival among the nations. Go back over some of these chapters and check the Scripture references. See if I am correct. Have I quoted the Scriptures accurately? Does the Bible really predict the return of Israel and the restoration of the Jewish people to faith? Is there a connection between their return and world evangelism?

If I am correct, then this information needs to be disseminated to every intercessor in the world. It will enable them to pray with more faith for the salvation of Israel and the nations. If these Scriptures have been accurately applied, then every mission agency and every missionary in the world need to know about this. These words from the prophets and apostles can be the source of a fresh infusion of faith for the success of their lives' work.

Even if you intend to continue reading, pause for a while until this information becomes revelation and a foundation for your life. Then let's consider in the next chapter how the Church is coming alive to a new love for Israel.

Notes

1. *Thayer's Greek-English Lexicon of the New Testament* (Grand Rapids, MI: Zondervan Publishing House, 1977), p. 168, s.v. "ethnos."
2. The word "missionary" is not used in Scripture.
3. Philip Jenkins, *The Next Christendom* (New York: Oxford University Press, 2002), p. 2.
4. The statistic about China comes from Floyd McClung, ed., *Light the Window: Praying Through the Nations of the 10/40 Window* (Seattle, WA: YWAM Publishing, 1999), p. 98. The 120 million believers is also a figure used by Brother Yun (see footnote 15) in his address to the participants at the International Christian Embassy Jerusalem's Feast of Tabernacles celebration that was held in early October 2004. Statistics from David B. Barrett and Todd M.

Johnson, *World Christian Trends AD 30–AD 2200* (Pasadena, CA: William Carey Library, 2001), p. 383, show an increase of over 70 million Christians from 1990 to 2000 in Latin America. The statistic about Africa also comes from Barrett and Johnson, *World Christian Trends.*

5. In *The New Christendom,* Jenkins cites the number of African Christians in 1900 as 10 million, compared to 360 million today (p. 4). The Christian History Institute estimates that there were approximately 8 to 9 million Christians in Africa in 1900, as compared to approximately 335 million today. http://chi.gospelcom.net/glimpsef/Glimpses/glmps151.shtml (accessed August 3, 2005).

6. J. Lee Grady, "Nigeria's Miracle," *Charisma* (May 2002), p. 40.

7. C. Peter Wagner and Joseph Thompson, *Out of Africa* (Ventura, CA: Regal Books, 2004), p. 13.

8. Ibid., p. 14.

9. Ibid., p. 188.

10. Ibid., pp. 37-38.

11. The World Factbook lists the population of Nigeria at approximately 128 million as of July 28, 2005. http://www.cia.gov/publications/factbook/geos/ni.html. Todd M. Johnson of the Center for Global Christianity gives the Christian population of Nigeria as 61 million. http: //www.globalchristianity.org (accessed August 2005).

12. David Garrison, *Church Planting Movements: How God Is Redeeming a Lost World* (Midlothian, VA: WIGTake Resources, 2004), p. 85.

13. Ibid.

14. Ibid.

15. Paul Hattaway, *The Heavenly Man: The Remarkable True Story of Chinese Christian Brother Yun* (London: Monarch Books, 2003), n.p.

16. Danyun, *Lilies Amongst Thorns: Chinese Christians Tell Their Story Through Blood and Tears,* trans. Brother Dennis (Kent, England: Sovereign World, 1991), n.p.

17. David Aikman, *Jesus in Beijing: How Christianity Is Transforming China and Changing the Global Balance of Power* (Washington, D.C.: Regnery Publishing, 2003), p. 285.

18. Ibid., p. 5.

19. Steve Cleary, "Over the Wall with the Gospel," *The Voice of Martyrs,* December 2004, p. 7. Used by permission of *The Voice of the Martyrs,* www.persection.com.

20. Ibid., p. 6.

21. Ibid., p. 7.

22. "The first missionary to Korea came off the passenger ship in 1869 and was 'bludgeoned to death 15 minutes after stepping on shore. It took a

Christian physician, Dr. Horace Allen, to establish the necessary beachhead which permitted the first Presbyterian, Horace Underwood, and the first Methodist, Henry Appenzeller, to enter Korea in 1884 and stay.'" Kenneth M. Scott, "Christian Medicine Abroad: A Place for You," *Journal of the Christian Medical Society*, Fall 1983, p. 10, quoted at Mission and Ministry: Christian Medical Practice in Today's Changing Culture. http: http://bgc.gospelcom.net/emis/vrekenmono/vreken1.htm.

23. Dr. James Anderson, "Korean Christianity: Persecuted, and Proud of It," CBC News Analysis and Viewpoint, January 5, 2005. http://www.cbc.ca/news/viewpoint/vp_anderson/20050105.html.

24. "Adamson Delivers Sound for the Faithful: Yoido Full Gospel Church," *Pro Audio Asia*, July/August 2003.

25. Geert Hofstede™ Cultural Dimensions, ITIM International, 2003 data. http://www.geert-hofstede.com/hofstede_south_korea.shtml.

26. Anderson, "Korean Christianity: Persecuted, and Proud of It."

27. Ibid.

28. Jeff Taylor, "Yearning to Be Free in Vietnam," *Charisma* (January 2002), p. 42.

29. David Garrison, *Church Planting Movements: How God Is Redeeming a Lost World* (Midlothian, VA: WIGTake Resources, 2004), p. 117.

30. Ibid., p. 99.

31. Ibid., pp. 111-122.

32. Ibid.

33. Thomas Boston, "Encouragement to Pray for the Conversion of the Jews" (sermon, 1716), quoted in Iain H. Murray, *The Puritan Hope: Revival and the Interpretation of Prophecy* (1971; repr., Carlisle, PA: The Banner of Truth Trust, 1998), p. 114.

34. James Rutz, *Megashift: Igniting Spiritual Power* (Colorado Springs, CO: Empowerment Press, 2005), pp. 5-6.

35. See Rutz, *Megashift: Igniting Spiritual Power*, chapter 1, "The New Kingdom Explosion: Exciting Miracles and Church Growth," with extensive footnotes.

36. Rutz, *Megashift: Igniting Spiritual Power*, pp. 9-12.

37. Jonathan Edwards, quoted in Murray, *The Puritan Hope: Revival and the Interpretation of Prophecy*, p. 154.

38. Norman Grubb, *Rees Howells: Intercessor* (Fort Washington, PA: Christian Literature Crusade, 1987), pp. 229-230.

39. Charles H. Spurgeon, *Metropolitan Tabernacle Pulpit* series of sermons, vol. 17, pp. 703-704, quoted in Murray, *The Puritan Hope: Revival and the Interpretation of Prophecy*, p. 256.

AWAKENING THE CHURCH
TO A LOVE FOR ISRAEL

If some of the branches have been broken off, and you,
though a wild olive shoot, have been grafted in among the others
and now share in the nourishing sap from the olive root, do not
boast over those branches. If you do, consider this: You do not
support the root, but the root supports you.

ROMANS 11:17-18

Pastor Ron Johnson and Bethel Temple Assembly of God in Hampton, Virginia, were experiencing a financial shortfall. His staff and church leaders asked the Lord for direction, but they heard nothing. Were they missing God somewhere? Was there correction He wanted to give? In times past, when a financial hardship had descended upon the congregation, God had been gracious to give them guidance, but this time the heavens seemed silent.

In the midst of their dilemma, Ron received a telephone call from the leader of a nearby Messianic Jewish congregation. "The Lord told me to call you," he said. "We are in a financial bind, and I believe you are supposed to help us."

Ron did not reply right away. *It seems to me that he has this thing in reverse,* Ron thought. *We need help, too. We certainly have no extra funds for anyone else.* Finally Ron gave a brief explanation of his church's circumstances: "Brother, we would love to help you, but we are having financial difficulties ourselves right now. I'm sorry, but I'm afraid there's not much we can do."

Satisfied that he had handled the request appropriately, Ron had no sooner replaced the phone in its cradle than he heard the voice of the Lord say, "Bless Israel!"

Wanting to be obedient, Ron called the Jewish leader back. "Let's meet for lunch to discuss your need," he said. "Even though we are in the same spot, this may be the Lord. Perhaps we can take a special offering for you."

A few days later, they sat together as Ron shared his plan: "We will set aside a Sunday to take the offering, and I will inform my congregation. You can visit us that day, and we'll see what the Lord has for you. We usually expect to collect $8,000, perhaps even $10,000 for special needs like this."

Ron was feeling very good about his decision as he made his way back to his car after lunch. He knew he had been obedient to the Lord, and he was hoping that the Lord would honor his obedience by breaking the financial deficit hanging over his own congregation. As he reached out to open the car door, he heard the still, small voice again: "Be extravagant!"

Now this sent Ron into a mental tailspin. "Lord, what do You expect us to do? You know we are in dire straits ourselves. How can we possibly be extravagant?"

No answer.

As Ron continued praying, he began to believe that they were to give the Messianic congregation a full Sunday's offering, which at the time, was about $50,000. He called his elders, told them of the conversations and asked them to be praying about it.

"We don't have to pray," was their response. "You have heard from God. Let's do it!"

Ron called his staff together and challenged them to curtail every unnecessary expense so that the full $50,000 could be saved within the next few weeks. On the day the check was to be given, the Messianic congregation was well represented, and their gratitude profuse. Ron's congregation had created a six-foot-long replica of the check to give to the visiting shepherd as a means of expressing their wholehearted approval of the celebratory blessing.

THE BLESSING OF BLESSING ISRAEL

Then it was Ron's turn to receive the blessing. "Now, Pastor," the visiting leader began, "let us pray with you and for you that God will supply all the financial needs of your own fellowship." With that, he proceeded to pray over Bethel Temple, concluding with the Aaronic benediction, a personally worded 3,500-year-old benediction that the Lord Himself had given Aaron through Moses for blessing all future generations of believers:

The LORD bless you and keep you;
the LORD make his face shine upon you and be gracious to you;
the LORD turn his face toward you and give you peace.[1]
Numbers 6:24-26

Soon after, an astonishing thing happened. In a little over a month, Bethel Temple had received *five times* the amount of the check *above their normal offerings!* Since that time, every January, Ron and his church have taken a special offering for a visiting Jewish ministry.

I met this anointed pastor and his delightful congregation when he chose the Messianic Jewish Bible Institute to be the recipient of that year's offering. He had extended an invitation to me to bring the messages at four worship gatherings that weekend. This time the church's offering was $67,000—the money to be used to train Jewish leaders in the former Soviet Union, in Latin America and in other nations.

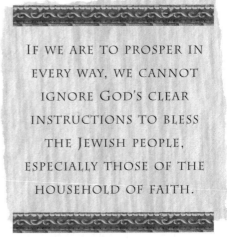

IF WE ARE TO PROSPER IN EVERY WAY, WE CANNOT IGNORE GOD'S CLEAR INSTRUCTIONS TO BLESS THE JEWISH PEOPLE, ESPECIALLY THOSE OF THE HOUSEHOLD OF FAITH.

Pastor Ron has learned a life-message: If we are to prosper in every way, we cannot ignore God's clear instructions to bless the Jewish people, especially those of the household of faith (see Gen. 12:1-3; Rom. 15:26-27; Gal. 6:10.)

ISRAEL'S HONORED ROLE

Another brother who has witnessed and received this promised blessing is Tom Hess. Each year near the time of the Jewish/biblical fall feasts,[2] Tom and his Jerusalem House of Prayer for All Nations host the All Nations Convocation, to which church leaders from around the world are invited. Often in attendance are leaders from the underground Church in China and Vietnam, from Eastern Europe, Africa and South America, and from many other nations—all of whom believe that our faith began and will culminate in Jerusalem and that the Jewish people and the nation of Israel are inextricably connected with all of this.

In 2002, one of the leaders attending Tom's convocation was

Bishop Jackson Khosa from South Africa. When Bishop Khosa learned that I would be visiting with Eitan and Connie Shishkoff at the Tents of Mercy congregation in the Kryot (an area of small towns) north of Haifa on the following *Shabbat* (Saturday), he asked if he could accompany me.

We enjoyed our time of worship with the congregation that Sabbath morning, and then we went to the Shishkoff home for a meal. After visiting for a while, we began to prepare for the return trip to Jerusalem, when Bishop Khosa said to Eitan and Connie, "May I pray for you before we leave?"

He drew near the couple and went to his knees, placing his hands on their feet. "I do not deserve to lay my hands upon your heads," he said. "You are our parents in the faith. Without your people we would never have known the one true God. My Bible says that in the last days, the hearts of the fathers will be turned to their children and the children's hearts to their fathers [see Mal. 4:6]. We turn our hearts to you. The Bible also says that if we honor our fathers and mothers, it will go well with us, and we will enjoy long life upon the earth [see Eph. 6:2-3]. I want all the blessings that God has to offer my people and me. We honor you, from whom all of us, as believers in Jesus, are descended." May the revelation that has come to this African bishop become evident to the whole Body of Messiah!

Similar to Bishop Khosa, Ram Zango, from Burkino Faso, has learned the importance of Gentiles honoring their Jewish fathers. Ram, a frequent visitor to Israel and to gatherings of Jewish and Gentile believers, participated in a meeting of Toward Jerusalem Council II in Vienna, Austria, in 2001.[3] As one of the Jewish brothers was about to bring a message, Ram left his seat in the audience and came to the front. After reading from the words of the prophet in Isaiah 49:23, he knelt before our Jewish brother and then, in a stunning act of humility, licked the dust from his feet.

"The prophet said that your former enemies will bow down and lick the dust at your feet," Ram said. "We are your former enemies, but now we honor you, the world's host people and the bringer of Israel's Messiah to all of us throughout the world."

The number of believers who have received revelation about Israel's honored role continues to grow. Believers from 12 island nations in the Pacific are in the process of building 12 large *waka* (very long canoelike boats), each of which will be able to carry 100 "Christian warriors." Their plan is to meet in New Zealand in 2006 in order to launch an 18-month evangelistic voyage to Israel. They will go ashore with this message from their distant islands: "We have come from the ends of the earth. We have heard and believe in your God. We have read your sacred Scriptures. We now believe in your Messiah and have come to honor you."

The underground Church in China, in the midst of revival, has raised up the Back to Jerusalem movement, which is training evangelists to reach the Muslim nations between China and Jerusalem. These steadfast believers know what it means to risk their lives for the faith. They are not deterred by the dangers. They understand that the Church's journey of faith began and will end in Jerusalem.

Coach Bill McCartney founded the Promise Keepers movement, which has swept across America and other nations, filling stadiums with its message to men to lead lives of love for God, for their wives and children and for their pastors and home congregations, and to seek reconciliation between denominations and races. In the midst of Coach McCartney's challenging Promise Keepers agenda, he became aware that the parent of all church divisions was the separation between Jews and Gentiles in the first centuries, when Gentiles became dominant in the

Church and began to turn their backs on their Jewish brothers and sisters.

Coach McCartney and Raleigh Washington have now started an organization called the Road to Jerusalem. Its intention is to awaken the Church to her alarming history of anti-Semitism and to challenge the Church to unite and bless the burgeoning Messianic Jewish movement as the resurrection of the original host "church."

Why, in our generation, are there so many like Pastor Ron, Bishop Khosa, Ram Zango, the Pacific Islanders, leaders from the underground churches in China and Vietnam, and Coach McCartney, who are suddenly turning their hearts to Israel and the Jewish people? Let me suggest again that it is an intersection of the promises of God with the fullness of time in which we live.

MEMBERS TOGETHER OF ONE FAMILY

Isaiah foresaw a time when Israel's Messiah would take "salvation to the ends of the earth" (49:6) and would bring "justice to the nations" (42:1). Ezekiel also knew of the impact that Israel would have on the nations (see 36:22-24), and the psalmist made it clear that all the nations would one day worship Israel's King and God (see Pss. 67:2; 72:17; 86:9; 98:2; 102:15).

Although Jesus' disciples did not comprehend what He was saying, Jesus assured His Jerusalem listeners, "I have other sheep that are not of this sheep pen. I must bring them also. They too will listen to my voice, and there shall be one flock and one shepherd" (John 10:16). Jesus was foreseeing the time when the Gentile nations would join the Jewish people as one flock.

The apostle Paul, who was called to carry the Name of Jesus "before the Gentiles and their kings and before the people of Israel" (Acts 9:15), knew that the Gentiles who would come to faith in Yeshua were not to remain separated from their Jewish brothers and sisters. "[Yeshua] has made the two one and has destroyed the barrier, the dividing wall of hostility" (Eph. 2:14), Paul told the church in Ephesus, in explaining that Jew and Gentile had been united as "one new man out of the two" (v. 15).

Paul assured the Ephesians that though at one time they, as Gentiles, had been "separate from Christ, excluded from the commonwealth of Israel, and strangers to the covenants of promise, having no hope and without God in the world" (2:12, *NASB*), they now had been brought near by the blood of Messiah and were "no longer foreigners and aliens, but fellow citizens with God's people and members of God's household" (v. 19).

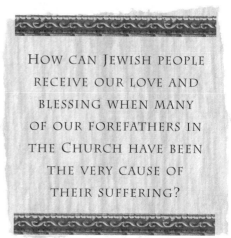

HOW CAN JEWISH PEOPLE RECEIVE OUR LOVE AND BLESSING WHEN MANY OF OUR FOREFATHERS IN THE CHURCH HAVE BEEN THE VERY CAUSE OF THEIR SUFFERING?

Notice that Paul did not say that Gentiles are citizens *instead of* Israel, which is what replacement theology teaches.[4] Rather, Paul said that we are *fellow citizens with* Israel. We non-Jews are now a part of the commonwealth of Israel; we are fellow citizens. As Americans, we can understand the concept of a commonwealth, since our nation originally was a part of the commonwealth of Great Britain. At that time, though we lived on American soil, our home country was England, our primary governing city was London, and our ruling sovereign was the king or queen of England.

In the same way, Paul declares that all non-Jewish believers in Jesus, the Jewish Messiah, are now a part of the commonwealth of Israel. We may be politically and geographically

American citizens—or Kenyans or Chinese or Brazilians—but if we are believers in Yeshua, our spiritual homeland is Israel, our principal earthly city is Jerusalem—which will one day receive the Jerusalem from above (see Rev. 21:2)—and our Supreme Ruler is the King of the Jews, Jesus, who will reign over God's one-world government (see Zech. 14:9).

Paul calls this a mystery: that the Gentiles are heirs *together*, members *together* and sharers *together* in the promise of God through Jesus (see Eph. 3:6). We have not replaced Israel; rather, we have become a part of her, members of her family. Not all of our new family members yet acknowledge their own Messiah, but we shall persevere in faith and in love until we see the entire family come to accept Him (see Rom. 11:26).

In Romans 11, Paul gives his olive tree analogy (more on this in chapter 11). Paul teaches that we are not to be arrogant in relationship with our yet nonbelieving Jewish brothers and sisters (see vv. 18-21). Rather, we are to look forward to the time when they will again be "grafted into their own olive tree" (v. 24).

SUMMARY

God's 400-year-old promise intersected with His timing at the burning bush as He prepared to lead Israel back to their Land of inheritance. Promise and timing collided again when Joshua was given the command to end Israel's 40-year desert experience and march into Canaan. A very clear intersection of promise and timing came during the latter days of the aging prophet Daniel when he read from the Jeremiah scroll and knew that the 70 years of Babylonian exile had come to an end. The supreme intersection of God's timing and promise was introduced that day in Nazareth when the angel Gabriel visited young Miriam. "You will be with child and give birth to a son," Gabriel announced. "He will be great and will be called the Son of the Most High. . . . [H]e will reign over the house of Jacob forever; his kingdom will never end" (Luke 1:31-33).

In more recent years there has come to us again an intersection of the promises of God with His timing. One singular event heralds that intersection—the ingathering of the nation of Israel from her 2,000-year exile. Israel's reentry as a nation onto the world's stage in 1948 was God's announcement that the season of the Messiah's return was beginning. The return to David's city, Jerusalem, 19 years later was God's further confirmation that everything was proceeding according to plan.

These two intersections form the backdrop of three other events that are shaping our twenty-first century: Jewish eyes are opening to the revelation that Yeshua is their Mashiach (Messiah); nations long held in darkness are learning of the God who brings redemption to the world through Israel's famous Son; and a centuries-long anti-Semitic Church is beginning to come alive to the Jewish roots of her faith, to acknowledge her sins and to come together with her Jewish brothers and sisters as one flock in God.

But this is a work in progress. Many questions have arisen about the events that have transpired and those yet to come. Daily challenges confront us. How are we to respond to God's work in the context of a terrorized world? How can Jewish people receive our love and blessing when many of our forefathers in the Church have been the very cause of their suffering? How can we genuinely bless the Jewish people who disagree with our faith in Jesus, while we joyously fellowship with those who have embraced it?

Such probing questions call for serious study and fervent prayer until the answers come. Let us walk together in search of them, keeping the following in mind:

When the promise of God and the timing of God intersect, there is a "suddenly" that causes a significant change in the world, and God begins to look for people who will participate with Him in what He is doing in that generation.

We are being offered the opportunity to join with God in His work in our day. Catch the wind of His breath. Learn His plan. Listen to His prophets. Look around you and watch Him at work. Become a willing participant in His end-time activity. And don't be afraid to ask questions!

Notes

1. The transliteration of this Aaronic blessing reads, "y'varechecha Adonai viyishmerecha, yaer Adonai panav elecha vichunecha yisa Adonai panav elecha v'yasem l'cha shalom."

2. The Jewish/biblical fall feasts begin on the 1st day of the 7th month of the biblical calendar with *Rosh Hashanah* (meaning "head of the year" and celebrated as the civil new year), followed by *Yom Kippur* (Day of Atonement) on the 10th day of the 7th month and ends with *Sukkot* (Feast of Tabernacles, also known as Feast of Trumpets), which begins on the 15th day of the same month and extends for 7 days. The spring feasts begin with *Pesach* (Passover) on the 14th day of the 1st month, followed by *Hag HaMatzah* (Feast of Unleavened Bread), which extends over the next 7 days, and ends with *Shavuot* (Pentecost) 50 days later.

3. The Toward Jerusalem Council II executive committee is a group of covenant brothers, Jews and Gentiles, who are praying and working toward the time when the universal Church will issue a reverse document to the one given after the first Jerusalem Council (see Acts 15). At that council, the Jewish apostles and leaders agreed to welcome Gentiles into the family of faith without the requirement that they become Jewish.

Toward Jerusalem Council II would say to the resurrected believing Jewish community of today, "Come on back. You are not required to become Gentile in your expression of faith. In fact, we who now welcome you back are your younger brothers in faith." Those of us on the committee carefully chose the title *"Toward* Jerusalem Council II," realizing that we have no authority to call such a council. We are committed to working with churches from a wide spectrum of Christian denominations as well as the evangelical/charismatic churches to point to the need and pray for the calling forth of such a council.

4. Replacement theology is the belief that the Gentile Church has replaced Israel, with the result that all the promises originally given to Israel now belong to the Church.

PART 2

QUESTIONS PEOPLE ASK ABOUT ISRAEL AND THE MIDDLE EAST

Many questions were asked of Jesus during the years of His public ministry. Some people who did not believe in Jesus were simply seeking justifiable reasons to arrest Him. Others were genuinely looking for answers. They wanted to know whether He was indeed the Promised Messiah of Israel. If so, why did He act the way He did? Why did He not declare Himself King and overthrow the Roman occupation forces?

His disciples, too, had their share of questions, often inspired by Jesus' own mysterious method of teaching. His messages were filled with parables that were intentionally designed to share the Kingdom message only with those whose hearts were open.

The reestablishment of the nation of Israel has also brought about a plethora of questions. Some of them come from people who do not believe that this regathering of Israel has anything to do with the purposes of God. Others come from people who believe the Prophets, but the timing of the return of the Jewish people and especially the return of the Jewish believers in Jesus call for a rearrangement of long-held theology, so these believers want answers. Others in the Church, who fully affirm their Messianic Jewish brothers and sisters, do not understand how we non-Jews are supposed to relate to recently established Messiah-believing synagogues. And how does all this affect other nations? Let us look at some of these often-asked questions.

CHAPTER 7

WHAT ABOUT THE ARABS?

*In that day Israel will be the third, along with Egypt and
Assyria, a blessing on the earth. The LORD Almighty will bless
them, saying "Blessed be Egypt my people, Assyria my
handiwork, and Israel my inheritance."*

ISAIAH 19:24-25

Appropriate love for Israel and the Jewish people does not negate
love for the Arab people, many of whom are also the descendants
of Abraham through his other sons and grandsons. Isaac
received the covenant blessing, as did his son Israel (Jacob); but
Ishmael, Esau and the sons of Keturah were also Abraham's
heirs. "They, too, must be considered when we hear the promise
that God made to Abraham: 'I will make you into a great nation
and I will bless you; I will make your name great, and you will be
a blessing. I will bless those who bless you, and whoever curses
you I will curse; and all peoples on earth will be blessed through
you'" (Gen. 12:2-3). Isaiah understood prophetically that at a
future time in history the Arab nations would be a blessing to
the whole earth (see 19:19-25).

IF IT IS TRUE THAT THE ARABS ARE TO BE A BLESSING AND TO RECEIVE GOD'S BLESSING, THEN WHY IS THERE SUCH HOSTILITY BETWEEN ARABS AND JEWS TODAY?

Abraham's wife Sarah had the idea that she would be able to
"build a family" by giving her maid Hagar to him (Gen. 16:2). As
soon as Hagar found that she was pregnant, however, Hagar
began to "despise her mistress" (v. 4). Then, when Sarah mis-
treated her, she fled. The angel of the Lord found Hagar and
gave her this prophetic word about her future descendants

through her son Ishmael: "I will so increase your descendants that they will be too numerous to count. . . . You are now with child and you will have a son. You shall name him Ishmael [which means "God hears"], for the LORD has heard of your misery. He will be a wild donkey of a man; his hand will be against everyone and everyone's hand against him, and he will live in hostility toward all his brothers" (vv. 10-12). There could hardly be a more accurate description of the history of the Middle East.

Ishmael's Blessing

Yet Ishmael, too, was to receive a blessing, for he, along with Abraham, received in his flesh the mark of the covenant. Abraham was circumcised at the age of 99; Ishmael, at 13. God promised Abraham that He would establish an everlasting covenant through his yet-to-be-born son Isaac, Sarah's firstborn; but He assured Abraham that Ishmael and his descendants would also be blessed: "As for Ishmael, I have heard you: I will surely bless him; I will make him fruitful and will greatly increase his numbers. He will be the father of twelve rulers, and I will make him into a great nation" (Gen. 17:20).

Note carefully the words "I will surely bless him." This may come as a shock to many of those who love Israel, but God does not intend for Ishmael's descendants to be denied their portion. This may account for the fact that more and more Arabs, many of whom have been followers of Islam for centuries, are coming to acknowledge the blessings that come to them through the promised Messiah, born through the lineage of their cousin Israel.

Even though Ishmael and his mother were sent away after Isaac's birth, they stayed in contact with each other; Ishmael and Isaac were together at the grave of Abraham (see Gen. 25:9). The descendants of Ishmael intermarried with Isaac's descendants and even held positions of importance in the nation of Israel.

David's sister Abigail married Jether the Ishmaelite (see 1 Chron. 2:17), and Obil the Ishmaelite was the keeper of David's camels when David was Israel's king (see 27:30).

That God intended Ishmael's descendants to be blessed can be further seen in the prophet Isaiah's specific references to some of the tribes of Ishmael when speaking of Israel as a light to the nations (see Isa. 42:11; 60:6-7; cf. Gen. 25:13-16). It may also be significant to note that the apostle Paul, in the earliest years of his walk as a believer, spent time in Arabia (see Gal. 1:15-17).

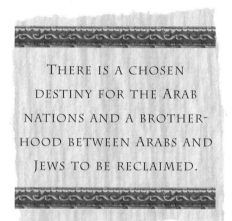

THERE IS A CHOSEN DESTINY FOR THE ARAB NATIONS AND A BROTHER-HOOD BETWEEN ARABS AND JEWS TO BE RECLAIMED.

In addition, the vast lands and oil reserves of this region provide evidence of God's intention to bless the sons of Ishmael. However, this blessing of natural resources has not yet been passed to the people; rather, they have been absorbed through the lavish lifestyles of many of the leaders.

Yes, in the midst of all the turmoil of the Middle East, there is a chosen destiny for the Arab nations and a brotherhood between Arabs and Jews to be reclaimed.

Father Wounds

In the spring of 1998, a group of Jewish and Gentile believers took a prayer journey through Spain, visiting many of the sites where decrees had been issued against the Jewish people and praying for both the Jewish people and the nations of the world. In Córdoba, we prayed in a cathedral that had once been a mosque. Afterward, we fell into conversation about the enmity between the sons of Ishmael and the sons of Israel. An insight of enormous significance began to surface in my consciousness.

I have witnessed in many children a great father wound—feelings of rejection and abandonment that have been caused by absentee or abusive fathers. As we talked in the cathedral that day, I began to see a parallel between these feelings and the Jewish-Arab estrangement prevalent today.

For 13 years Ishmael had been the favored son of his father, Abraham. Abraham had yearned for a son, but Sarah's womb was barren. Sarah intervened, Hagar conceived, and Ishmael was born. Even though God kept telling Abraham that Ishmael was not the "son of promise," it would likely have been impossible for this man who had yearned for a son to hold back normal fatherly affection. It is not hard to imagine Abraham's delight and Ishmael's joy as they walked side by side through the boy's early years, until Ishmael was ready to celebrate his entrance into manhood.[1]

Then, just as Ishmael was entering into young adulthood, another son appeared. That fact would have been difficult enough, but when Abraham agreed to Sarah's demand that Ishmael be sent away, the agony and rejection in Ishmael's heart would have been immense. Ishmael married and had 12 sons, as did his nephew Jacob (Israel) a few years later.

We moderns are very aware of the effect of childhood trauma—how we carry wounds into our adulthood, wounds that affect the way we relate to our wives, our children, our surroundings. We also know that the stories of childhood are passed on to succeeding generations, who often take up the offense of past injustices. We need only think of the grim family histories of generations of Native Americans and African-Americans or the lingering damage suffered by the children of Nazi Holocaust survivors. If families are not reconciled, then the stories of the past become legends that shape a people, each succeeding generation identifying with, perhaps even magnifying, the atrocities of the past.

Today millions of Ishmael's descendants carry a father wound that has been intensified by centuries; the result is an inexplicable anger and hatred in the hearts of the Arab people— a sense of injustice in relationship to their Jewish cousins that no longer knows rational cause.

Abraham had six other sons, born to him through his later marriage to Keturah: Zimran, Jokshan, Medan, Midian, Ishbak and Shuah (see Gen. 25:1-4). Only Midian's descendants figure significantly in further biblical history, unless Jokshan's son Sheba is the same Sheba from which the famous queen at the time of Solomon was descended. These six sons were sent "away from his son Isaac to the land of the east," while "Abraham left everything he owned to Isaac" (vv. 5-6), thereby declaring that none of the other sons were legitimate heirs. Even though Abraham was a man of great wealth, Keturah's sons, like Hagar's son, received only gifts. These other sons of Abraham were always considered second-class family members, "sons of his concubines" they are called (v. 6), even though Scripture also clearly identifies Keturah as his wife (see v. 1). It is easy to assume that the progenies of these six sons figure into the mix of today's hostile Arab nations.

Isaac's other son, Esau, and his descendants, who came to be known as the Edomites, bring another complicating factor to the Middle East. Edom occupied much of the territory from the Dead Sea to the Red Sea and the Sinai Peninsula, and were often at enmity with their Israelite cousins. Although their kingdom had ceased to exist by the time of Jesus, they appear prominently in the Gospels as the Herodians, who were descended from Herod, a son of Esau. Esau's exact descendants are unknown today, yet the rivalry between Esau and his twin brother, Jacob (Israel)—the trickery, deceit and hatred—live on in their offspring. The blood of Syria, Assyria, Persia, Egypt, Moab and Ammon (sons of Lot) is also a part of these complex societies, now intermingled so that no bloodline has remained pure through the centuries.

ARE THERE SPECIFIC PROPHETIC PROMISES MADE TO THE ARABS, THE SONS OF ISHMAEL?

Yes, the sons of Ishmael and Israel's neighbors figure significantly into God's end-time plans. Isaiah describes a time yet in the future when Egypt and Assyria, along with Israel, will be a blessing on the earth. What was Assyria in Isaiah's day includes parts of Turkey, Iraq and Syria today. By substituting the names of these present-day countries, we come up with a remarkable Scripture as it relates to today's Arab world:

> In that day [an expression often used to denote the time of the end] there will be an altar to the LORD in the heart of Egypt, and a monument to the LORD at its border. It will be a sign and witness to the LORD Almighty in the land of Egypt. . . . The LORD will make himself known to the Egyptians, and in that day they will acknowledge the LORD. . . . In that day there will be a highway from Egypt to Assyria [Turkey, Iraq and Syria]. . . . The Egyptians and the Assyrians [Turks, Iraqis and Syrians] will worship together. In that day Israel will be the third, along with Egypt and Assyria [Turkey, Iraq and Syria], a blessing on the earth. The LORD Almighty will bless them saying, "Blessed be Egypt my people, Assyria [Turkey, Iraq

and Syria] my handiwork, and Israel my inheritance" (Isa. 19:19-25).

In the last several years, we have begun to see the promises found in this Scripture fulfilled. Christians have gathered together in Arab nations. Even before the fall of Saddam Hussein in 2003, there was a Christian leaders' conference to which I was invited in Baghdad. Unfortunately, I was not able to attend. Although the conference may have been sparked by Saddam Hussein's desire to present the façade of Christian freedom in Iraq, it was used as an opportunity for some of my friends to pray at one end of the "highway" between Egypt and Assyria.

My friend Homer Lanier told me of a similar visit to Cairo, Egypt, the other end of the highway, where Christians were praying. Homer saw a wood burning of the Isaiah 19:23-25 passage hanging on the wall of one of the families he visited. Homer said, "Sometimes my colleagues of many years, Michael and Alis Niebur [who live in Israel], invite people from overseas to expose them to 'Isaac,' while Mimi and I host some of them in Lebanon to introduce them to 'Ishmael.' In this way, we hope to share our 'Two-Eyed Vision' with believers who will have God's heart for both people."[2] Homer's two-eyed vision is God's love for Israel and His love for the Arabs.

Many Egyptian Christians, along with other Christians in the Middle East, are burdened to pray for the families of both Ishmael and Isaac. Early in 2004, I spent a blessed week with the Gateways Beyond discipleship school, located on the island of Cyprus. This Jewish-led training school brings together Jews and non-Jews who pray fervently for the reuniting of the sons of Abraham. A few days earlier I had spent time with a Palestinian Christian leader whose heart throbs with love, not only for his Arab brothers (who are often maligned and misunderstood), but also for his Israeli cousins and fellow relatives in the family of Jesus. In addition, in the past few years there have been a number of planned gatherings between Messianic Jews and Palestinian Christians who are determined to break down walls of hatred and to learn to love each other.

No, the destiny of the Arab world is not forgotten; God's plan is that the Arabs enter their fullness in the kingdom of God.

Yet they, just as all the nations of the earth, must come to God through a Jew, the Jewish Messiah, as Jesus told the Samaritan woman at the well (see John 4:22). God did not send us Americans an American Messiah. Nor did He send the Africans an African Messiah or the Chinese a Chinese Messiah. The same is true for the Iranians, the Syrians and the Saudis. All of us must come to God through the Jewish Messiah.

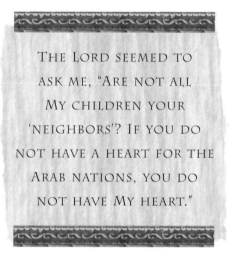

THE LORD SEEMED TO ASK ME, "ARE NOT ALL MY CHILDREN YOUR 'NEIGHBORS'? IF YOU DO NOT HAVE A HEART FOR THE ARAB NATIONS, YOU DO NOT HAVE MY HEART."

Another friend of mine lives and works among the Muslims in France, where he often finds receptive hearts. When these Muslims come to acknowledge Jesus as Savior and Redeemer, he leads them in this prayer of repentance: "I receive Jesus, the Jewish Messiah, as my Savior and Lord." He tells how these new believers at first almost choke on the words, but then their grimaces turn into grins and finally into laughter as they respond with joy.

"You no longer have to talk to them about loving the Jews or about 'replacement theology'," my friend says. "They know that they have come to faith through a Jew and that God's hand is still upon this covenant people."[3]

———

When the nations come to the conclusion of their pilgrimage and enter into the eternal Kingdom, they won't have become so enmeshed that they have lost their unique identities. God loves diversity. Each nation or tribe will bring its own gifting to the table of the Lord. John the Revelator envisioned every tribe, language, people and nation represented when we all assemble before the throne of God (see Rev. 5:9).

My friend John Dawson (the international president of the world's largest missions organization, Youth With A Mission) has traveled the nations as much as any person I know. He enjoys the cultures of the world and delights to see the giftings of the nations used to glorify God. He foresees the time when the Arab nations will bring to the Lord's table their extraordinary gifts. Their special gift of hospitality is one gift they may bring. (Anyone who has ever been invited into a Bedouin tent or an Arab shop or home will understand this.) Their sense of honor will also serve them well among the redeemed community of nations.

WHAT ABOUT ALL THE CHRISTIANS WHO SEEM TO HAVE BECOME SO OBSESSED WITH ISRAEL?

I understand these fellow Christians. When we begin to grasp God's prophetic regathering and His end-time purposes for Israel, we may take up an offense for this centuries-long persecuted people and lose touch with the heart of God for all people. As I began to learn more about the atrocities of the Church toward the Jewish people, and as I became acquainted with more and more Jewish believers, my love for them grew, so much so that I began to take up the offense of the Jewish people and found little love in my heart for the Palestinians and Israel's other enemies.

But the Lord arrested me on several occasions. "How can you be a part of My solution if you turn your back on some of My people?" He seemed to ask. "Have I changed the first and second commandments, loving God with all your heart, soul, mind and strength, and loving your neighbor as yourself? Are not all of My children your 'neighbors'? Now I want you to get acquainted with more of My Arab children, those who already believe in Me and those who do not yet believe. If you do not have a heart for the Arab nations, you do not have My heart."

It is true that in God's eyes, Jerusalem is "set in the center of the nations" (Ezek. 5:5). Even the boundaries of nations are somehow inextricably bound to the "number of the sons of Israel" (Deut. 32:8). God in His Word does not speak of Israel in the same way that He speaks of all other nations; with Him it is always "Israel . . . and all the other nations" (Jer. 36:2; see also Ezek. 28:25). Nations come to know Him as God through His dealings with Israel (see Ezek. 37:28; 38:16; 39:7) and will be judged by how they treat this chosen nation (see Joel 3:2).

Just as Israel had its own unique call from God, so also the times and boundaries of the nations were foreordained by the Almighty. The transformed Babylonian king Nebuchadnezzar became quite confident that the "Most High is sovereign over the kingdoms of men and gives them to anyone he wises" (Dan. 4:25). John calls Jesus the "ruler of the kings of the earth" (Rev. 1:5). No nation escapes His ultimate control.

Similarly, Paul assured the Athenians that, even if they did not recognize God, it was He who "determined the times set for them and the exact places where they should live" (Acts 17:26). Why? Paul says that "God did this so that men would seek him and perhaps reach out for him and find him" (Acts 17:27). In other words, just as God is at work to bring about the ultimate destiny of Israel, so He is orchestrating everything to bring about His ultimate witness to all the nations.

Today the nations of the world are in turmoil. Our question is not so much, Why is this happening? as it is, What doors are opening through these international changes? In God we have a heart for all His children. We are committed to the chosen family of Israel, but we know that God's intention is to embrace and save all the nations of the earth.

HOW CAN JEWISH PEOPLE, WHO HAVE KNOWN HORRENDOUS PERSECUTION THROUGH THE YEARS, BE SO AGGRESSIVE AND UNCARING TOWARD THEIR PALESTINIAN NEIGHBORS?

To be sure, not all Israelis act kindly toward their Arab neighbors. The pressure of living in conflict for many years has taken its emotional toll on both Arabs and Israelis. However, it is also true that the world media does not paint an accurate picture of the conflict and is often quick to point its finger at Israel. Several examples illustrate this unfortunate reality.

On September 30, 2000, the *New York Times* displayed a picture of an Israeli soldier, billy club in hand, standing over a person who had obviously been beaten. The caption beneath the picture read: "An Israeli policeman and a Palestinian on the Temple Mount." Dr. Aaron Grossman from Chicago, Illinois, saw the picture and wrote a letter to the editor of the *Times*:

Regarding your picture on page A5 of the Israeli soldier and the Palestinian on the Temple Mount—that Palestinian is actually my son, Tuvia Grossman, a Jewish student from Chicago. He and two of his friends were pulled from their taxicab while traveling in Jerusalem, by a mob of Palestinian Arabs, and were severely beaten and stabbed.[4]

In the spring of 2002, after Palestinians had murdered innocent Jewish people during the Passover celebration in Netanya, the Israeli army sent troops into Jenin, a known harbor for homicide bombers. Without investigation, the world media began calling it the Jenin Massacre. Later, when the United Nations' investigation found no such massacre, the news media barely reported the correction.

Also in the spring of 2002, *USA Today* ran a full-page article about Hadassah Hospital in Jerusalem. The article, "All Wounds Treated the Same at Hadassah," describes the treatment of 20-year-old Israeli Cpl. Sammy Nabuani, who had been confined to his hospital bed since the night, two months earlier, when a Palestinian man shot him as he stood guard at the biblical site of Rachel's Tomb just outside Bethlehem. Next to him lay a 31-year-old Palestinian man who was shot by Israeli soldiers during the siege of Bethlehem's Church of the Nativity. Since the hospital's opening in 1912, it has had a policy of treating all patients alike, no matter what their politics, religion and ethnicity are. Israeli soldiers and other citizens are treated in the same hospital, often in the same room as the terrorists who tried to kill them.[5]

This kind of story rarely makes the news (the *USA Today* article being an exception). Israelis are not all saints, but never does the Israeli army intentionally send its soldiers into Arab territory to kill innocent civilians, nor does the government of Israel move into Arab villages to provoke altercations.

The day of peace between Israel and Ishmael will come. The prophets foresaw it. But it will not be a peace carved out by compromise and treaties—that kind will be broken. Peace will come at last through the returning and reigning Messiah. In the meantime, the conflict over the Land continues to rage.

Notes

1. Today, when a young man reaches the age of 13, he undergoes a ceremony known as a *Bar Mitzvah*. It is a celebration of his becoming a "son of the covenant" (the translation of "Bar Mitzvah"), and it signifies his entering into manhood. During this ceremony, the young man will usually be "called to the Torah" for the first time, which means that he is invited to read from the Torah and he often will bring a brief homily of the Torah reading that is scheduled for the week of his Bar Mitzvah.

2. Homer Lanier, personal communication. Used by permission.

3. Personal conversation with a friend from France in Jerusalem, 2002. Used by permission.

4. "The Photo That Started It All," *HonestReporting.com*, October 20, 2000. http://www.honestreporting.com/articles/45884734/reports/The_Photo _that_Started_it_All.asp (accessed July 11, 2005).

5. Vivienne Walt, "All Wounds Treated the Same at Hadassah," *USA Today*, May 10, 2002. http://www.usatoday.com/news/world/2002/05/10/hospital.htm (accessed July 11, 2005).

DOES THE LAND STILL BELONG TO ISRAEL?

He is the LORD our God; his judgments are in all the earth.
He remembers his covenant forever, the word he commanded, for a
thousand generations, the covenant he made with Abraham, the oath
he swore to Isaac. He confirmed it to Jacob as a decree, to Israel as an
everlasting covenant: "To you I will give the land of
Canaan as the portion you will inherit."

1 CHRONICLES 16:14-18

No other country in the world can boast of a deed signed by the Almighty Himself. When God gave Abraham's descendants the Land, the Land was inhabited by Kenites, Kenizzites, Kadmonites, Hittites, Perizzites, Rephaites, Amorites, Canaanites, Girgashites and Jebusites; and it would not become the inheritance of Israel for another 400 years (see Gen. 15:13,19-21). The "sin of the Amorites [had] not yet reached its full measure" at the time God spoke the promise to Abraham (v. 16); therefore God, in His justice, could not yet give Abraham the Promised Land. When the 400 years had ended, God called Moses, and later Joshua, to lead Israel's descendants to conquer the Land by driving out its inhabitants and destroying every vestige of idolatry (see Num. 33:51-53).

WAS THE ALMIGHTY ASKING HIS CHOSEN FAMILY TO COMMIT GENOCIDE—TO DESTROY A WHOLE RACE OF PEOPLE?

God's sense of timing and judgment are not the same as ours. The Lord said through Isaiah, "My thoughts are not your thoughts, neither are your ways my ways" (Isa. 55:8). When the sins of a nation are ripe, God judges that nation.

God sent a flood to destroy Noah's generation. This was

obviously the single most devastating event that civilization had ever experienced, yet God knew that the time for judgment had come. Later, though God had been patient with Israel for years, even centuries, the time came for Israel's judgment. God sent foreign powers, some of whom were themselves evil, to conquer and subdue her.

Shortly before this latter judgment, the prophet Habakkuk, appalled at the evil in his own land, cried out, "How long, O LORD? . . . Why do you make me look at injustice? Why do you tolerate wrong?" (Hab. 1:2-3).

God's answer to Habakkuk was precise, but shocking: "Look at the nations and watch—and be utterly amazed. For I am going to do something in your days that you would not believe, even if you were told. I am raising up the Babylonians, that ruthless and impetuous people" (1:5-6).

NO OTHER COUNTRY IN THE WORLD—EXCEPT ISRAEL—CAN BOAST OF A DEED SIGNED BY THE ALMIGHTY HIMSELF.

When Habakkuk realized what God was saying—that God was going to use Babylon to punish Judah—it was more than he could comprehend. "O LORD, are you not from everlasting? . . . Why are you silent while the wicked swallow up those more righteous than themselves? . . . Is he [the wicked foe] to keep on emptying his net, destroying nations without mercy?" (1:12-13,17).

When no answer was forthcoming, Habakkuk mused, "I will stand at my watch and station myself on the ramparts; I will look to see what he will say to me, and what answer I am to give to this complaint" (2:1).

Jesus indicated in His parable of the wheat and tares that the end of the age will come when both wickedness and righteousness have ripened throughout the earth (see Matt. 13:24-30,36-43; more on this in chapter 9). At that point, the wicked will be thrown "into the fiery furnace, where there will be weeping and gnashing of teeth" (v. 42), or as John describes in his revelation, "into the great winepress of God's wrath" (Rev. 14:19).

Judgment is not a subject that we moderns enjoy. We love to speak of the love and mercy and patience of the Lord, all of which are real. But there comes an end to God's forbearance. Judgment *will* come!

Ethnic cleansing, when humankind targets a people group for destruction—whether that annihilation is leveled against the Armenians, the Sudanese, the Jews or any other of a number of ethnic groups that have borne the brunt of unjust governments—is one of the darkest blots in human history. But when God decides that the wickedness of a nation is ripe, it is His prerogative to judge and even to destroy. Obviously, the Canaanites at the time of Joshua, with their human sacrifices, idolatry and gross immorality, had reached the point of no return; and God thus commanded Joshua and the Israelites to take no prisoners. That's not a solution we like to accept.

SURELY YOU DON'T BELIEVE THAT GOD HAS GIVEN ISRAEL A JOSHUA-TYPE COMMAND IN OUR DAY. RIGHT?

No, Israel has no such command from God, nor have I ever heard of any Israeli who would make such a claim. Israel simply wants to live at peace in her ancient homeland. However, the situation in Israel is the exact opposite. The surrounding nations desire to push Israel into the sea.

The maps used by Arab nations do not, even today, acknowledge Israel's existence. In the textbooks of Arab schools, the entire land of Israel is still considered to be occupied territory, and thus, land to be reclaimed. Hundreds of thousands of Jewish people were driven from Arab lands during the early years of Israel's return from the nations (just as they were driven from Spain and Portugal and from many other countries throughout their history). Meanwhile, today hundreds of thousands of Arabs live peacefully in the State of Israel, many with voting privileges with which they elect Arab members of the Knesset, Israel's legislature.

The contrast between the actions of the Jews and the Arabs is astonishing, yet the Jews are the ones being accused of ethnic cleansing. In fact, one of America's best-known Christians, in describing the conflict between the Palestinians and the Israelis, is so misinformed about the situation that he says, "They're [evangelical Christians who believe that today's Israel has a right to the Land] really advocating ethnic cleansing. There's no justification for that in Scripture."[1]

I am one of those who advocate Israel's right of return to the Land, based on both prophecy and the vote of the United Nations. I have fellowshipped for years with those who have a similar understanding of Scripture, yet I have never heard any Jewish person, either in Israel or in the Diaspora, advocate ethnic cleansing of the Palestinians. In fact, the prophets make it quite clear that aliens (non-Israelis) have a right to live in the Land and should be treated as equals to Jewish citizens, as long as they understand that the Land, on the basis of God's promise, belongs to Israel (see Ezek. 47:22-23).

IN SCRIPTURE, ISRAEL WAS ALLOTTED ALL THE TERRITORY FROM THE EUPHRATES RIVER IN THE EAST, TO LEBANON IN THE NORTH, AND TO EGYPT IN THE SOUTH. WILL ISRAEL EVER HAVE THIS ENTIRE TRACT OF LAND?

God's promise to Abraham was this: "To your descendants I give this land, from the river of Egypt to the great river, the Euphrates" (Gen. 15:18; see also Deut. 1:7; 11:24; Josh. 1:4). God's promise was unconditional. The Land belongs to the people of Israel today and has belonged to them through all the years of their exile. When the people of Israel began to return, they were returning to the Land given to them by God through the patriarchs. Much like Hosea had to buy his wife Gomer back from the slavery into which she had sold herself (see Hos. 3:1-3), as early as the late nineteenth century, Jewish benefactors and foundations began to buy land so that early Jewish settlers could establish themselves in the Land—all in anticipation of their ultimate return.

Yet to Moses, God clarified the issue of possession. Although the Land belonged to the people of Israel in perpetuity, they would only continue to live there if they remained faithful to Him. Moses predicted,

> If you do not obey the LORD your God and do not carefully follow all his commands and decrees I am giving you today, . . . the LORD will cause you to be defeated before your enemies. The LORD will drive you and the king you set over you to a nation unknown to you or your fathers. You will have sons and daughters but you will not keep them, because they will go into captivity. You will be uprooted from the land you are entering to possess. Then

the LORD will scatter you among all nations, from one end of the earth to the other (Deut. 28:15,25,36,41,63-64).

The history of Israel is written in these words of Moses. Biblically, the Land belongs to Israel, but her total possession of the Land depends on her faithfulness to God. Ezekiel makes it clear that the return from the nations would happen not because the worldwide descendants of Israel had at last become a righteous people but because God chose to prove His faithfulness to them as a nation. Full possession of the Land awaits their return to the Lord.

It is not for your sake, O house of Israel, that I am going to do these things [bring you back], but for the sake of my holy name, which you have profaned among the nations where you have gone. I will show the holiness of my great name (Ezek. 36:22-23).

HAS THE UNITED STATES COME UNDER A CURSE BECAUSE WE HAVE ENCOURAGED ISRAEL TO PULL BACK FROM JUDEA AND SAMARIA AND OTHER LANDS ALLOTTED BY GOD TO ISRAEL?

In modern times, the land of Israel was divided under the British Mandate (British military rule of Ottoman territory in Palestine between World War I and World War II). Britain, after an initial consideration of making Israel's homeland the entire tract of land promised to Israel in Scripture, compromised by forming an Arab State (Transjordan, which is today's Jordan) to the east of the Jordan River, leaving the land to the west for the State of

Israel. Further compromises were made until Israel was given only a small percentage of the biblical land allotted, and even then a war had to be fought to secure it.

Through the prophet Joel, God has warned that He will judge the nations for scattering the people of Israel and dividing their Land:

> In those days and at that time, when I restore the fortunes of Judah and Jerusalem [that certainly sounds like the twentieth and twenty-first centuries!], I will gather all nations and bring them down to the Valley of Jehoshaphat. There I will enter into judgment against them concerning my inheritance, my people Israel, for they scattered my people among the nations and divided up my land (Joel 3:1-2).

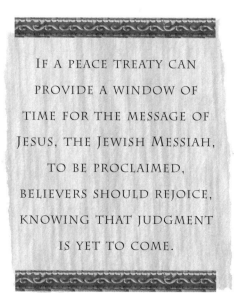

IF A PEACE TREATY CAN PROVIDE A WINDOW OF TIME FOR THE MESSAGE OF JESUS, THE JEWISH MESSIAH, TO BE PROCLAIMED, BELIEVERS SHOULD REJOICE, KNOWING THAT JUDGMENT IS YET TO COME.

So when our American presidents participate in dividing up the Land, they may be making the wrong decision biblically, while making the right decision prophetically. Let me explain. Biblically, the Land belongs ultimately to Israel, and nations are brought into judgment for dividing that land. However, Daniel spoke of a covenant that would be made, but not kept (see Dan. 9:27). The pressure from the West may force Israel into that treaty-to-be-broken when all the nations gather against Jerusalem (a peace treaty will one day be signed, but it will be a temporary peace prior to the time that all the nations gather against Jerusalem; see Zech. 12:3; 14:2). However, if such a peace treaty can provide a window of time for the message of Jesus, the Jewish Messiah, to be proclaimed both in Israel and in the surrounding nations, we believers should rejoice, even knowing that judgment is yet to come.

Yes, the Land belongs to Israel by decree of God. But no, Israel will not possess all of the Land until the nation returns to the Lord—at which time the kingdom will be restored to Israel and David's Son will return to rule, anticipating a yet future time when the "kingdom of the world has become the kingdom of our Lord and of his Christ, and he will reign for ever and ever" (Rev. 11:15).

Note

1. Tony Campolo, quoted in Joseph Farah, "Bearing False Witness," *The Washington Times,* June 28-July 4, 2004, national weekly edition. Tony Campolo is professor emeritus of sociology at Eastern University in Pennsylvania.

Will Jesus Literally Reign as King on Earth?

They asked him, "Lord, are you at this time going to restore the kingdom to Israel?" He said to them: "It is not for you to know the times or dates the Father has set by his own authority."

ACTS 1:6-7

I am continually amazed at how childhood experiences and early learning can leave their imprints on our lives, even into old age. Certain foods we ate or songs we sang in preschool may bring back images that trigger emotional responses when we are in our 70s. If we have been privileged to grow up in a nurturing home, most of those responses will be positive. If life was hard in our younger years, we will have more to overcome.

This same thing holds true regarding belief systems that were a part of our early history. We may understand intellectually that certain beliefs are not valid, but our emotional responses often take years of training to unlearn. Several biblical doctrines, or beliefs, that I was taught in the church of my youth had to be abandoned when I began to search the Scriptures for myself. Some of those beliefs, nonetheless, held emotional attachments that for me were difficult to break.

Strangely enough, one of these doctrines was that Jesus would never set foot on the earth again. To this day, I have no idea how my teachers explained Zechariah 14:3-4, which reads,

> Then the LORD will go out and fight against those nations, as he fights in the day of battle. On that day his feet will stand on the Mount of Olives, east of Jerusalem, and the Mount of Olives will be split in two from east to west, forming a great valley, with half of the mountain moving north and half moving south.

In fact, I don't even remember seeing that verse. But now it is obvious to me that the Lord will indeed return to the earth, because the Mount of Olives was not split in two the first time He came.

IS IT NOT POSSIBLE THAT ZECHARIAH 14:3-4 IS REFERRING TO JESUS' COMING THE FIRST TIME AND TO A SPIRITUAL EARTHQUAKE THAT HAS ALREADY OCCURRED?

Though it is clear to me from Zechariah 14:3-4 that Jesus must come again to the earth, not everyone agrees. Some interpreters of the Bible suggest that these verses refer to Jesus' first coming, when a spiritual earthquake would have occurred. I believe that they are forgetting an important principle of Biblical interpretation.

That important principle is this: Always assume that Scripture is to be taken literally unless there is clear reason for a more figurative, or spiritualized, understanding. Of course, there are some passages that obviously require a figurative interpretation, which is the case in John 1:29, where John the Baptist calls Jesus the Lamb of God. John was not saying that Jesus was a literal lamb, but rather that Jesus was God's Lamb to be slaughtered for the sins of the world. On the other hand, when Micah speaks of Bethlehem as the place out of which will come a ruler who will shepherd God's people Israel, he is referring to a literal city and a literal ruler (see Mic. 5:2-5). There may be a spiritual message in a prophetic passage, but a literal fulfillment would still be awaited.

Zechariah's prophecy continues, "On that day living water will flow out from Jerusalem, half to the eastern sea and half to the western sea, in summer and in winter. The LORD will be king over the whole earth. On that day there will be one LORD, and his name the only name" (vv. 8-9).

About verses 8 and 9, some interpreters propose a figurative interpretation so that "living water" refers to life in the Spirit and that Jesus' reign as "king over the whole earth" is a spiritual reign that is occurring now.

However, that interpretation does not fall in line with what I see Zechariah very specifically saying about this coming of the King. Zechariah prophesies that all the nations will gather for battle against Jerusalem (see 14:2). Such a battle has not yet taken place, though the votes in the United Nations often indicate that the time may be near. Zechariah proclaims in verse 2, "Half of the city will go into exile," which is something that the U.N. is pushing for even now. The Lord will come forth to fight against the nations. When his feet touch down on the Mount of Olives, the mountain will split in two, forming a valley that will lead into the now-closed Eastern Gate (see Zech. 14:3-4; Ezek. 44:1-3), which is, interestingly enough, just as the geological fault line on the Mount of Olives predicts. Living water will flow from Jerusalem (see Zech. 14:8; Ezek. 47:1-12) and the Lord will be King of the whole earth (see Zech. 14:9).

But Zechariah's is not the only prediction of Jesus' return to the earth. On the day of Jesus' ascension, two angels assure the apostles, "This same Jesus, who has been taken from you into heaven, will come back *in the same way* you have seen him go into heaven" (Acts 1:11, emphasis added). Ezekiel, at another time, hears very clearly that the Temple Mount is the exact location where the throne will be located and the place that will receive the soles of the Lord's feet (see Ezek. 43:6-7). We look forward to the day when these prophecies are fulfilled, when Jesus comes again.

IF THERE IS TO BE A LITERAL KINGDOM UPON THE EARTH, THEN WHY DID JESUS SAY NOTHING ABOUT IT?

In order to understand the answer to this question, we need to realize that Jesus *did* speak about a literal earthly kingdom. Even though Jesus often used the expression "kingdom of heaven" and "kingdom of God," the ears of Israel, because of their familiarity with the words of the prophets, heard "kingdom of God upon the earth." Zechariah declares not only that the Lord will be king over all the earth (see 14:9) but also that the Lord will "return to Zion and dwell in Jerusalem" (8:3) and build the Temple, where He will sit and rule on His throne (see 6:13) and where "survivors from all the nations that have attacked Jerusalem will go up year after year to worship the King, the LORD Almighty" (14:16). Ezekiel agrees with Zechariah's prediction that God will rule on His throne, saying, "This is where I will live among the Israelites forever" (Ezek. 43:7). Much of the last part of Ezekiel's prophecy describes the new Temple area and Temple (see Ezekiel 40–47). Since these passages describe the Temple very specifically, it would take some wrestling with Scripture to explain them away.

Jesus spoke constantly of His kingdom, but we have so spiritualized His message that we have failed to consider the domain over which He is to reign. The Kingdom was a constant thread in Jesus' teaching ministry from beginning to end, as it also was in the message that John brought in preparing for the arrival of his cousin. "Repent, for the kingdom of heaven is near" were the first words spoken by both John and Jesus as they began to minister (Matt. 3:1; 4:17). The Gospel writers continually describe Jesus' ministry as one in which He preached the good news of the Kingdom (see Matt. 4:23; 9:35; Luke 4:43; 9:2; 12:32).

Jesus was a master storyteller, often speaking in parables. Why? In order to disguise the "knowledge of the secrets of the kingdom of heaven" (Matt. 13:11) in a way that those who were destined to receive it could do so, while hiding this knowledge from others. "The kingdom of heaven is like" seems to be one of Jesus' favorite introductions to His stories. His parables of the wheat and the weeds (see v. 24), the mustard seed (see v. 31), yeast (see v. 33), the treasure in the field (see v. 44), the merchant looking for fine pearls (see v. 45), the net full of fish (see v. 47), the storehouse of new and old treasures (see v. 52), the two debtors (see 18:23), the landowner and the workers (see 20:1) and the wedding banquet (see 22:2) are all introduced in exactly the same way, and thus are "Kingdom parables" that would have brought images of Zechariah and Ezekiel or other prophets.

Some of Jesus' Kingdom parables clearly predict a going away and a coming back. In Matthew 25, the 10 virgins are waiting for the bridegroom. The purchase price has been paid. The groom has gone to prepare the home, while the bride and the bridal party prepare themselves for his return (see also John 14:3). All of this refers to Jesus' sacrificial offering with which He bought His bride (see 1 Cor. 6:19-20; 1 Peter 1:18-19) and His return to heaven, where He would wait for His time to come back to the earth (see Acts 3:21).

Both the parable of the talents and that of the 10 minas speak of a master who gives gifts and then leaves, only to return years later to find out what his servants have done with their gifts. Luke says that the 10-minas parable was given to people who "thought that the kingdom of God was going to appear at once" (Luke 19:11). Matthew's account of the parable of the talents says that the master was going on a journey (see Matt. 25:14) and that "after a long time the master of those servants returned and settled accounts with them" (v. 19). All of these stories predict a return of the Master to His people, and thus the return of Jesus to the earth to reign as King. In these parables, we also see certain of the King's servants assigned a domain over which they rule, one servant over 10 cities, another over 5 (see Luke 19:17,19).

Jesus' Kingdom messages were not confined to parables. The Kingdom belongs to "the poor in spirit" and to "those who are persecuted because of righteousness," He told the crowd on the mountainside early in His public appearances (Matt. 5:3,10). "Seek first his [the Father's] kingdom and his righteousness," He later added, "and all these things [the necessities of life] will be given to you as well" (6:33). "Your Father has been pleased to give you the kingdom," Luke records Jesus as saying (Luke 12:32); and when asked to teach His disciples how to pray, He replied, "Your kingdom come, your will be done

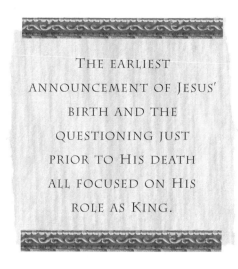

THE EARLIEST ANNOUNCEMENT OF JESUS' BIRTH AND THE QUESTIONING JUST PRIOR TO HIS DEATH ALL FOCUSED ON HIS ROLE AS KING.

on earth as it is in heaven" (Matt. 6:10). It is significant to note that this well-known prayer calls forth the kingdom of God to the earth: "Your kingdom come . . . on earth." John sees this finally and ultimately accomplished when heaven joins the earth and God dwells again with His people (see Rev. 21:1-3); yet this aged apostle also refers to a thousand-year reign of Jesus upon the earth. During this time, not only is Jesus King, but also some of the resurrected saints will come to life, will be seated on thrones and "given authority to judge" in the King's administration (v. 4).

But there is more about this *King* that our ears have been too dull to hear. The earliest announcement of Jesus' birth and the questioning just prior to His death all focused on his role as King. "The Lord God will give him the *throne* of his father David, and he will *reign* over the house of Jacob forever; his *kingdom* will never end," the angel Gabriel told Mary, on the night of the visitation (Luke 1:32-33, emphasis added). "Where is the one who has been born *king* of the Jews?" the wise men asked months later (Matt. 2:2, emphasis added), prompting Herod's questions about prophecies concerning his birth. "In Bethlehem in Judea," they replied (v. 5), before quoting Micah the prophet (see Mic. 5:2): "But you, Bethlehem, in the land of Judah, are by no means least among the rulers of Judah; for out of you will come a *ruler* who will be the shepherd of my people Israel" (Matt. 2:6, emphasis added). These verses refer to Jesus' role, not only as Savior, but also as King—King of Israel.

Over 30 years later, Jesus stood before Pilate and heard the question, "Are you the king of the Jews?" to which He replied, "Yes, it is as you say." All three of the Synoptic Gospels, Matthew, Mark and Luke, record this noteworthy conversation (see Matt. 27:11; Mark 15:2; Luke 23:3). The Gospel of John supplies additional remarks from Jesus to Pilate: "You are right in saying I am a king. In fact, for this reason I was born, and for this I came into the world" (John 18:37).[1]

Even though Jesus kept talking about the *Kingdom,* the disciples still had many questions, especially regarding timing—as evidenced by their last conversation before His ascension: "Lord, are you at this time going to restore the kingdom to Israel?" (Acts 1:6). Jesus answered this question by telling them about all the things that must transpire before His return to reign. "You will receive power when the Holy Spirit comes on you; and you will be my witnesses in Jerusalem, and in all of Judea and

Samaria, and to the ends of the earth" (Acts 1:8). In other words, "The entire world must first learn of Me before I return to reign in Jerusalem as King over a restored kingdom of Israel."

"This gospel of the kingdom will be preached in the whole world as a testimony to all nations, and then the end will come," He had told them a few days earlier (Matt. 24:14), but the disciples obviously did not comprehend, not even after the outpouring of the Holy Spirit on Shavuot (Pentecost) a few days later. Otherwise, Peter's vision of the four-cornered sheet with the menagerie of unclean animals and reptiles would have been unnecessary (see Acts 10:9-23). In Peter's house-top vision in Joppa, the Lord was opening the heart of this Jewish apostle to spread the gospel to the nations.

Yes, Kingdom teaching was an essential part of the message of both Jesus and His apostles. "We must go through many hardships to enter the kingdom of God," Paul and Barnabas told the new believers in Lystra, Iconium and Antioch (Acts 14:22). In Ephesus, Paul spoke boldly for three months, "arguing persuasively about the kingdom of God" (Acts 19:8), and later in Rome, "boldly and without hindrance he preached the kingdom of God" (28:31). Yet all this emphasis on the Kingdom has often been divorced from the place where He is to return to reign.

WHY IS AN EARTHLY REIGN SO IMPORTANT? WHY CAN WE NOT JUST GO TO HEAVEN AND REMAIN WITH HIM IN HEAVEN WHERE HE LIVES?

The victory that the devil scored in the Garden gave him authority over the earth, an authority and rule intended for Adam and his descendants. Jesus acknowledged the devil's authority when He called him "the prince of this world" (John 14:30), a prince that was to be driven out as He, Adam's "son," paid the price of redemption for the family and regained the ground, even the literal ground, that God had originally given His "father" Adam in the Garden (see John 12:28-32). Paul called the devil "the ruler of the kingdom of the air" (Eph. 2:2) and referred to Jesus as "the last Adam" (1 Cor. 15:45). "For since death came through a man [Adam], the resurrection of the dead comes also through a man [Jesus]. For as in Adam all die, so in Christ all will be made alive. . . . Then the end will come, when he hands over the kingdom to God the Father after he has destroyed all dominion, authority and power," Paul wrote (vv. 21-22,24) " 'The first man Adam became a living being'; the last Adam, a life-giving spirit" (v. 45).

The devil understood this conflict. This is the reason he was trying to win the victory by offering Jesus a shortcut to the earthly kingdom. As he showed Jesus "all the kingdoms of the world," he said to Him, "All this I will give you . . . if you will bow down and worship me" (Matt. 4:8-9). Luke's version of the devil's promise reads, "I will give you all their authority and splendor, for it has been given to me, and I can give it to anyone I want to" (Luke 4:6). This was a legitimate offer, except that receiving the bribe would have placed Jesus under the devil's control, as it had the first Adam, so that nothing would be gained.

But by passing the test, Jesus declined to accept the devil's inappropriate offer of the kingdoms of the world; He did not reject the kingdoms of this world, but instead refused them on the conditions presented. As a descendant of Adam who had no sin of His own, Jesus was able to bear up under the sin of the whole family and redeem the earth as well as the earth's intended family of rulers. Isaiah saw this sacrifice clearly:

> He [Jesus] was pierced for our transgressions, he was
> crushed for our iniquities; the punishment that brought

us peace was upon him, and by his wounds we are healed. . . . [T]he LORD has laid on him the iniquity of us all. [T]he LORD makes his life a guilt offering. . . . [M]y righteous servant will justify many. . . . [H]e poured out his life unto death, and was numbered with the transgressors. For he bore the sin of many, and made intercession for the transgressors (Isa. 53:5-6,10-12).

Jesus' death was essential for the retaking of the earth. Adam lost domain of the earth by submitting to the enemy. Adam's Greater Son paid the family debt in order to regain the lost territory and give it back to its rightful heirs—those made in His (God's, Jesus') image. Jesus' reign upon the earth is not because He is the Son of God—that only gives Him heavenly authority. His reign upon the earth is as the Son of Adam and the Son of David—the Son of Man. As born-again family members of this Son of Man, we are given shares in the family inheritance—in the Kingdom (consider again the full impact of Luke 12:32).

ARE YOU SAYING THAT JESUS WAS ALWAYS SPEAKING OF A LITERAL EARTHLY KINGDOM?

No, during Jesus' three-year teaching ministry, there were three aspects of the restoration of the Kingdom that were still in the future: (1) the coming of the Kingdom through the outpouring of the Holy Spirit at Pentecost (see Acts 2:1-4), which ultimately spread to all believers; (2) the return of the King to reign over the earth from Jerusalem; and (3) the eternal Kingdom, when heaven and Earth are joined and "the kingdom of the world [becomes] the kingdom of our Lord and of his Christ, and he will reign for ever and ever" (Rev. 11:15).

Prophetic language often has multiple fulfillments. Isaiah's prediction that "the virgin will be with child and will give birth to a son, and will call him Immanuel" (Isa. 7:14) happened first when Isaiah "went to the prophetess, and she conceived and gave birth to a son" (8:3) named Maher-Shalal-Hash-Baz. Eight hundred years later, Matthew quotes from Isaiah to show the prophecy's ultimate fulfillment in the birth of Jesus, called Immanuel, just as Isaiah had foreseen (see Matt. 1:22-23).

Everything the prophet sees is described as transpiring in the future, even though centuries may elapse between the realization of one part of the prophecy and its completion. Isaiah described Jesus as One who will "come up from the stump of Jesse" and upon whom "the Spirit of the Lord will rest" (Isa. 11:1,2), all of which happened at His first coming. But then Isaiah says, "He will strike the earth with the rod of his mouth; with the breath of his lips he will slay the wicked" (v. 4), as though this,

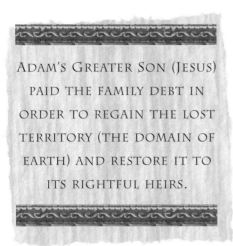

ADAM'S GREATER SON (JESUS) PAID THE FAMILY DEBT IN ORDER TO REGAIN THE LOST TERRITORY (THE DOMAIN OF EARTH) AND RESTORE IT TO ITS RIGHTFUL HEIRS.

too, would happen at the same time. The apostle John, writing decades after Jesus lived on the earth, knew that a portion of the Isaiah prophecy took place at His first coming, but that this last part would happen at His next arrival (see Rev. 19:15).

These predictions of the future reign of Jesus upon the earth and in eternity future after death has been destroyed are not always easily distinguishable. Nor is it always easy to determine when the prophets are speaking of the battle at the beginning of the earthly kingdom, when the devil is bound for a thousand years (see Rev. 20:1-3), and when they are speaking of the one reserved for the end of those thousand years, when the devil is banished forever (see 20:7-10).

IS NOT THE MESSIAH'S KINGDOM ALREADY HERE? IF HE IS KING, THEN THERE IS ALREADY A KINGDOM.

One day in Caesarea Philippi, Jesus told His disciples, "Some who are standing here will not taste death before they see the Son of Man coming in his kingdom" (Matt. 16:28; see also Mark 9:1). The Pharisees heard Jesus' teaching on the Kingdom and wanted to know when the Kingdom would come. He replied, "The kingdom of God does not come with your careful observation, nor will people say, 'Here it is,' or 'There it is,' because the kingdom of God is within you" (Luke 17:20-21). The Kingdom is now, within us, as the King rules in us. Paul twice referred to our bodies as temples of God in which He dwells (see 1 Cor. 3:16; 6:19). There is a future restoration of God's kingdom to the earth; but even now, while we wait for that to occur, we can begin to embody His kingdom on the earth.

Bill Johnson's book *When Heaven Invades Earth* speaks not about the New Jerusalem coming down from God out of heaven but about God's kingdom producing His work through us now by His Spirit. As we walk in His authority, we bring an aspect of the kingdom of heaven to the earth today. For example, Bill tells of a fortune-teller who came to his town as a part of a Fourth of July celebration. Since there are no fortune-tellers in heaven, Bill set out to remove this one from his domain. "You don't exist in heaven; you are not to exist here," he prayed. "This is my town. You are here illegally. I forbid you to establish roots here!"[2] Bill was not speaking to the woman, but rather to the spirits. He did not even speak loudly enough for her to hear; nor did he go near her tent—but the fortune-teller left town the next morning. Bill was learning how to bring heaven to the earth even now. Our lives become beachheads from which the coming Kingdom can invade parts of the earth in this day, anticipating the later total takeover when the rightful King returns.

WHERE IN THE BIBLE CAN ONE FIND THE BEST DESCRIPTIONS OF THE FUTURE REIGN OF THE MESSIAH?

The most fascinating descriptions of the millennial reign are found in Isaiah and Zechariah and in parts of John's Revelation. John saw "an angel coming down out of heaven, having the key to the Abyss and holding in his hand a great chain. He seized the dragon, that ancient serpent, who is the devil, or Satan, and bound him for a thousand years . . . to keep him from deceiving the nations anymore until the thousand years [are] ended" (Rev. 20:1-3).

This binding of the devil will happen when the skies open and a Man on a white horse, accompanied by all the armies of heaven, makes His descent to the earth (see Rev. 19:11-14). This time His entrance into our atmosphere will not come through the angel Gabriel's visit to an unknown teenager in Nazareth; He will come through the clouds as Conquering King to reign. "Every eye will see him," says John, "even those who pierced him; and all the peoples of the earth will mourn because of him" (Rev. 1:7).

The nations have raged against Him and will be united to strike a final blow to the "people of the covenant" in Jerusalem (see Ps. 2 and Zech. 12:3; 14:2), but it will not happen. According to Zechariah, this whole era will be ushered in just at a time when it looks as if Jerusalem is doomed and Israel will finally be annihilated. All the nations will be gathered to fight against Jerusalem. When Israel appears to be trapped is the very time that the clouds will open and the King will return to "fight against those nations," accompanied by "all the holy ones" (Zech. 14:3,5). John calls these holy ones "the armies of heaven" (Rev. 19:14), and Paul describes this same scene as the revelation of the Lord Jesus "from heaven in blazing fire with his powerful angels" (2 Thess. 1:7). We obviously are speaking of both angel hosts and the returning saints.

From Isaiah's account it seems that "in that day" (Isa. 11:11) there will still be battles to be fought on Israel's eastern and western borders in the territories of Philistia on the west and Edom and Moab on the east. But "the LORD will dry up the gulf of the Egyptian sea; with a scorching wind he will sweep his hand over the Euphrates River. He will break it up into seven streams so that men can cross over in sandals. There will be a highway for the remnant of his people that is left from Assyria, as there was for Israel when they came up from Egypt" (vv. 15-16).

After all this happens, nature will break forth in praise. Isaiah paints a superb picture of wolves, lambs, lions, goats, leopards, bears and calves all frolicking together (see Isa. 11:6-7; 65:25). Children will claim lions, leopards and wolves as playmates (see 11:6). Never since the Garden will creation have lived in such harmony. All those groaning prayers from creation will be answered (see Rom. 8:22).

I tell my grandchildren, "When that day comes, you jump on a lion, I'll jump on a tiger, and we'll race!" We will all be friends. "For the earth will be filled with the knowledge of the glory of the LORD, as the waters cover the sea," the prophet Habakkuk says (2:14), agreeing with Isaiah (11:9). This glory will fill the earth because the King will be on the earth again, this time as reigning Sovereign.

There is an amazing story of the town of Almolonga, Guatemala, which has experienced some of these Isaiah-blessings after a large percentage of the people turned to the Lord. At one time, all four jails in this town of about 20,000 residents were full, because of the high rate of alcoholism and crime. The crops had all but dried up. People lived in poverty. Then the revival came. In the next few years, 18,000 people turned their lives to the Lord, all the jails were closed, and the whole countryside was so affected that officials from the Agriculture Department of Guatemala sent representatives to see what had caused the transformation. Carrots, cabbages and other produce increased to proportions never before seen, and the harvests were so frequent that new trucks and equipment had to be purchased to bring the crops to market. The citizens of Almolonga have established a Kingdom beachhead on the earth and are experiencing a foretaste of life in the millennium![3]

This millennial reign of the King will introduce an era of peace when no weapons of warfare are needed. Swords will be made into plowshares and spears into pruning hooks (see Isa. 2:4), so completely will wars have ceased. The streets will be filled with the joy of brides and bridegrooms and people bringing thank offerings to the Lord (see Jer. 33:11).

Ben-Gurion Airport will not be large enough, nor the streets and highways wide enough, to accommodate all the global visitors who will annually travel to Jerusalem to celebrate the feasts and to worship the King (see Zech. 14:16-17). This glorified Jesus will be "clothed with majesty and will sit and rule on his throne" inside the grandest Temple of all time, one that He Himself will build (see Zech. 6:13). Beside Him, seated on 12 thrones, will be the 12 apostles "judging the twelve tribes of Israel" (Matt. 19:28).

This whole scenario will open up with a stream of living water that will flow out from Jerusalem all the way down to the

Dead Sea, leaving everything in its wake alive and fresh. Fishermen will be able to stand along the shore and fish, and fruit trees on the banks will bear fruit each month, just as John later predicted (see Ezek. 47:8-12; Zech. 14:8; Rev. 22:2).

The Lord returns as King of the Jews, but also as King of the Nations, and Head of a One-World Government with headquarters, not in Brussels or New York, but in Jerusalem, ushering in a world peace that will last for a thousand years. But this is not eternity.

THERE IS A FUTURE RESTORATION OF GOD'S KINGDOM TO THE EARTH, BUT WHILE WE WAIT, WE CAN BEGIN TO EMBODY HIS KINGDOM ON THE EARTH.

WHO WILL BE LIVING DURING THE MILLENNIAL REIGN?

Zechariah says that those who will be alive during the millennial reign include "survivors from all the nations that [had] attacked Jerusalem" (Zech. 14:16) in the earlier battle. John says that these survivors will be joined by those who are a part of the first resurrection (see Rev. 20:6). Paul says, "The dead in Christ will rise first. After that, we who are still alive and are left will be caught up together with them in the clouds to meet the Lord in the air" (1 Thess. 4:16-17). These resurrected saints will have new bodies, which likely will be similar to Jesus' body during the 40 days He appeared to His disciples after His resurrection and before His ascension.[4] These survivors from the nations, in their natural bodies, will marry, have children, and live long lives (see

Isa. 65:20-22). Since the devil will be bound at this time, there will be no demonic activity, but we will still be subjects of our own fallen nature. Sin and sickness, death's companions, though lessened, will still be a part of life, until the end of the millennium, when these, too, are thrown into the lake of fire (see Rev. 20:14).

Although the thousand years will be a time of unprecedented peace and glory, a dark cloud will still lie ahead. There will be one last battle to fight. The devil will be released and will be allowed one last attempt to deceive and to pervert the image of God in humankind. Those who will have come to faith during the millennium must undergo their own testing before their enemy is banished and God's presence is forever established.

WHERE MAY I FIND CLEAR BIBLICAL DESCRIPTIONS OF ETERNITY FUTURE?

John describes the last battle and the ultimate victory in the last two chapters of his Revelation. Satan will be released "for a short time" (Rev. 20:3) and will go out "to deceive the nations in the four corners of the earth . . . to gather them for battle" (v. 8). A vast army will surround Jerusalem again, similar to the one a thousand years earlier, but fire will come down from heaven and devour them (see v. 9). The devil will be "thrown into the lake of burning sulfur, where the beast and the false prophet had been thrown," where "they will be tormented day and night for ever and ever" (v. 10).

Paul speaks of this time as a time when all that is perishable will be clothed with the imperishable and the mortal with immortality (see 1 Cor. 15:53). Those who are still alive will be changed into their resurrection bodies (see v. 51), and "death [will be] swallowed up in victory" (v. 54). Paul says that when the end comes, Jesus will "[hand] over the kingdom to God the Father after he has destroyed all dominion, authority and power. For he must reign until he has put all his enemies under his feet. The last enemy to be destroyed is death" (vv. 24-26). The redeemed will be ushered into the eternal city, where the Jerusalem from above joins Jerusalem below. "I saw a new heaven and a new earth," John says.

> I saw the Holy City, the new Jerusalem, coming down out of heaven from God . . . And I heard a loud voice from the throne saying, "Now the dwelling of God is with men, and he will live with them. They will be his people, and God himself will be with them and be their God. . . . The old order of things has passed away . . . I am making everything new!" (Rev. 21:1-5).

The eternal city will still bear the imprint of those who have been used in redemption. Carved into the foundation stones and the gates of this New Jerusalem for all eternity will be the names of the tribes of Israel and those of the 12 Jewish apostles (see Rev. 21:12,14). Lest we think that this eternal city will have nothing to do with the earth, John makes it clear that there will still be nations and there will still be kings of the earth (all submissive subjects of "the King") who bring their glory and honor to the city (see v. 26).

Adam's family will be back where it started, except that this time "no longer will there be any curse" (Rev. 22:3). Just as Adam and Eve saw God's face in the Garden, so we will "see his [God's] face" (v. 4) and will enter into our full destiny of rulership and authority under the Lord and the Lamb, reigning with Him eternally (see v. 5) on an earth that will have been joined to heaven. "To him who overcomes, I will give the right to sit with me on my throne, just as I overcame and sat down with my Father on his throne" (3:21), Jesus told the Laodiceans. Sit with Him on His throne? This is pretty heady business!

Some years ago Paul Billheimer began to grasp some of this and wrote a book called *Destined for the Throne*, in which he describes man's present pilgrimage as preparation to reign as the Bride of the Lamb. "This world is a laboratory in which those destined for the throne are learning in actual practice how to overcome Satan and his hierarchy," Billheimer wrote, before making this startling statement:

> This means that *redeemed humanity* outranks all other orders of created beings in the universe. Angels are created, not generated. Redeemed humanity is both created and generated, begotten of God, bearing His "genes," His heredity. Through the new birth a redeemed human being becomes a bona fide member of the original cosmic family, "next of kin" to the Trinity.[5] Thus God has exalted redeemed humanity to such a sublime height that it is impossible for Him to elevate them further without breaching the Godhead. This is the basis for the divine accolade of Psalm 8:5: "Thou hast made him but little lower than God" (ASV *and Amplified*).[6]

Lest we become puffed up by Billheimer's interpretation of Scripture, let us remember that this is a call for unmitigated humility and that pride disqualifies us. Our only response must be praise and worship to the One who has chosen and qualified us.

WHEN PETER SAYS THAT JESUS MUST REMAIN IN HEAVEN UNTIL THE TIME COMES FOR HIM TO RESTORE EVERYTHING OF WHICH THE PROPHETS SPOKE (SEE ACTS 3:21), IS HE REFERRING TO THE MILLENNIUM OR TO THE ETERNAL CITY?

Both! There are at least five basic conditions of Jesus' return that were lost in the Garden and that await their ultimate restoration: (1) close communion with God; (2) intimacy with each other; (3) our authority to rule over the earth; (4) Spirit power and communication; and (5) the purity and pristine beauty of the earth. All five of these conditions already have a measure of restoration in and to those of us who have received and walk in the Spirit. A further restoration will occur in the millennial kingdom, but the ultimate restoration will only be reached in eternity future, when God and humankind are fully restored to each other.

1. *Close communion with God.* The Genesis account describes a time when God could be heard "walking in the garden [where Adam and Eve dwelt] in the cool of the day" (3:8). Adam and Eve had no problem hearing and understanding God (see 1:28-30; 2:15-17). They were in such intimate fellowship that God actually brought the animals and birds to Adam so that he could name them (see v. 20). The Fall changed things radically; Adam and Eve "hid from the LORD God among the trees of the garden" (3:8). Yes, there is a restoration to close communion with God now through our rebirth in the Spirit, but it will not reach its intended magnitude until we enter into

the eternal city, the restored Garden.

2. *Intimacy with each other.* After Creation, there was such transparency of life between Adam and Eve, such intimacy of spirit, that they knew no shame, even in their nakedness. But sin had its effect. Adam blamed Eve, Eve blamed the serpent, and even the angels were likely not allowed to record the accusatory conversation that must have taken place between these two lovers as they were banished from their celestial home (see Gen. 3:12-13,23-24)! A fog came between these two friends and lovers, a fog that still clouds fellowship between fellow human beings. Yes, we learn to love and forgive, to confess and to forbear, in restored fellowship between us, but this is only a foreshadowing of the fellowship that awaits us in our future resurrected bodies.

3. *Authority to rule over the earth.* "Rule" was the order for Adam in his unspoiled state—"over the fish of the sea and the birds of the air, over the livestock, over all the earth, and over all the creatures that move along the ground" (Gen. 1:26). But there was no more ruling over nature after the Fall. Now he had to work the ground from which he had been taken (see 3:1-15,23) and fall prey to the one who had orchestrated his demise. Yes, Jesus has given us authority through the outpouring of the Holy Spirit, but the perfection of our authority to rule over the earth will only be reached in eternity future.

4. *Spirit power and communication.* At Creation, God breathed into Adam the very life of God Himself (see Gen. 2:7) so that he had within himself the breath of God. But at the Fall, the spirit within him was sepa-

rated (see Gen. 2:17) from the Spirit of God. Biblical death is separation, in this case a separation of God's Spirit from man's spirit. Only when we are born again of the Spirit is this connection between God and us restored. The human spirit, in communion with God, was intended to be the "control panel" of the human anatomy. But at the Fall, when our spirits were cut off from His Spirit, we were left with "soul control," being controlled not by the Spirit but by the mind, will and emotions. From that day forward, we have presumed that if our minds are educated, our wills directed and our emotions under control, we can live victoriously. This was never intended to be. The Germany of World War II possessed all of these elements, but became only an educated, arrogant, strong-willed, depraved nation. Yes, walking in the Spirit gives us Spirit power, but the fullness of this exchange is yet future.

5. *The purity and pristine beauty of the earth.* Humankind's sin affected not only our own future but also the future of every form of life on the entire planet. Because of that sin, the world tumbled into turmoil. The whole animal kingdom became subject to disease and death. We were intended to be their master and protector, but because we gave that authority to our enemy, the whole planet has fallen into decay.

"The earth will wear out like a garment," Isaiah warns us (51:6). Paul said to the Romans, "The whole creation has been groaning as in the pains of childbirth right up to the present time" (8:22), yearning to be "liberated from its bondage to decay and brought into the glorious freedom of the children of God"

(v. 21). I sometimes tell people that their pets earnestly desire that they get themselves together so that the animals, too, can live in perfect peace. A return to the Lord will have its effect upon the earth even now (remember the story of Almolonga, Guatemala); and yes, during the millennium the whole animal kingdom will enjoy life as never before since the Garden, but not until the complete return of a state of purity will creation fully thrive again.

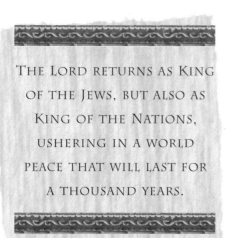

THE LORD RETURNS AS KING OF THE JEWS, BUT ALSO AS KING OF THE NATIONS, USHERING IN A WORLD PEACE THAT WILL LAST FOR A THOUSAND YEARS.

WHEN SHOULD WE EXPECT THE GREAT TRIBULATION?

It seems, from what the prophet Daniel says, that the signing of a peace treaty may mark the beginning of the greatest upheaval of all time (see Dan. 9:27). Daniel called it a "time of distress such as has not happened from the beginning of nations until then," assuring his readers also that "At that time your people . . . will be delivered" (12:1). Jesus referred to Daniel's prophecy, agreeing that this "great distress" would be "unequaled from the beginning of the world until now—and never to be equaled again" (Matt. 24:21). This time of anguish has been predicted repeatedly by both prophets and apostles. Jeremiah describes an awful day like no other, "a time of trouble for Jacob, but he will be saved out of it" (Jer. 30:7). This time of terrifying upheaval will also be God's time of great purification. Malachi sees the Lord suddenly coming to His Temple (see 3:1), and then says, "But who can endure the day of his coming . . . For he will be like a refiner's fire" (v. 2).

Paul had some of the clearest thoughts on this whole time period. He spoke of the day when the Lord would return, saying, "That day will not come until the rebellion occurs and the man of lawlessness is revealed, the man doomed to destruction. He will oppose and will exalt himself over everything that is called God or is worshiped, so that he sets himself up in God's temple, proclaiming himself to be God" (2 Thess. 2:3-4).

In recent years much of the Church has believed that we non-Jewish believers will be taken from the earth before this period of intense suffering. In my book *Your People Shall Be My People*, I mention a simple study that I did with three Greek words: *thlipsis,* translated "tribulation" as well as "distress," "persecution," "hardship" and "trouble"; and two words for "wrath," *orge* and *thumos.* By looking at each of the passages in which these three words occur, I came to the conclusion that we are never assured from either Jesus or the apostles that we will escape thlipsis. On the other hand, Scripture is very clear that no believer experiences the wrath of God (see 1 Thess. 5:9; Rom. 5:9).[7]

Believers in many nations have experienced suffering so intense that it would be meaningless and offensive to try to speak to them about escaping the great tribulation. Our brothers and sisters in China and in many other nations are even today being tortured in indescribable ways. This is thlipsis, but it is not at the hand of God; it is not God's wrath. We learn from the book of Job that God may allow things that He does not send, but He will use it all for our own perfection and good (see Job 1—3; 42:12).

With Jesus' parable of the wheat and tares, He informs us that two things will happen as we move toward His return. The wickedness of the world will ripen to the point of harvest. But at the same time righteousness will mature (see Matt. 13:24-30). This is an extremely important end-time picture. There are those who believe that the world will get worse and worse as we move toward the coming of the Lord. They are correct. Others have thought that the people of God will become more and more powerful as we approach the Lord's return. They, too, are correct. Jesus lets us know in this parable that both wickedness and righteousness must increase side by side as we near the harvest. When John sees the angels going out to reap, it is because "the harvest of the earth is ripe" (Rev. 14:15). Both wickedness and righteousness are growing ripe for harvesting. God will not judge the world until its wickedness is ripe, but He will also not reward the saints until righteousness is ripe.

The most wicked days the earth has known are ahead, along with the grandest days for the people of God. This clash of cultures between those who are walking in the Lord and those who have chosen a path of evil will escalate. "Then the righteous will shine like the sun in the kingdom of their Father," Jesus said (Matt. 13:43), quoting Daniel's picture of the end-times. Five hundred years earlier, the Lord had told Daniel, "Those who are wise will shine like the brightness of the heavens, and those who lead many to righteousness, like the stars for ever and ever" (Dan. 12:3). Then He cautioned Daniel, "Close up and seal the words of the scroll until the time of the end. Many will go here and there to increase knowledge" (v. 4). This is a pretty amazing description of the time in which we live, when millions of us are in the air or on our superhighways going "here and there" at every moment of every day and night. "Many will be purified, made spotless and refined," Daniel tells us, "but the wicked will continue to be wicked" (12:10).

Why is this parable so important? Because we believers need to be prepared for great evil and yet be expectant of great righteousness, as wickedness and righteousness mature simultaneously.

HOW DOES THE RAPTURE RELATE TO JESUS' RETURNING TO THE EARTH TO REIGN? AT WHAT POINT DO WE RISE TO MEET HIM IN THE AIR?

First of all, let me be quick to assure you that as long as we are in the body, all of us only "know in part" (1 Cor. 13:9). Having said that, it seems to me that we have placed too much emphasis on the Rapture, as though we are taken away to be with the Lord forever, when in fact, He is returning to the earth to reign. Is it possible that our "rapture" is only as we go out to meet Him at the time He is returning, much the way an entourage goes out to meet a visiting dignitary that is about to make a grand entrance? The midnight cry to the 10 virgins was, "Here's the bridegroom! Come out to meet him!" (Matt. 25:6). Their purpose in going to meet him was to bring him back, not to remain where they met him. Similarly John records that after Lazarus' death, as Jesus was nearing Bethany, "she [Martha] went out to meet him" (John 11:20). She went not to stay outside the city but to bring Him in to her place. Is it too much of a stretch to assign this meaning to Paul's Thessalonian letter?

"God will bring with Jesus those who have fallen asleep in him," Paul said, referring to Jesus' return (1 Thess. 4:14). "The Lord himself will come down from heaven" (v. 16). Notice the Lord comes *down!* At the same time, however, we "who are still alive and are left will be caught up together with them [the resurrected saints] in the clouds to meet the Lord in the air.

And so we will be with the Lord forever" (v. 17). Why would we go up if He is coming down? Obviously, we go up to meet Him only to return with Him as in the illustrations above.

In the meantime, those who die—who "depart and [are] with Christ" (Phil. 1:23)—are forming a great cloud of witnesses, cheering us on from the grandstands (see Heb. 12:1). It is quite possible that, since Jesus is now interceding for us and since we believers are a part of His body (see Rom. 8:34; 1 Cor. 12:27), the departed saints are even now joining Jesus in intercession on our behalf as they also await the time when they will appear with Him in His glory (see Col. 3:4).

All this heightens my anticipation of the future. But I must remember there is still much to be done. The world is in transition. I must remember not to sit and wait, but to participate with Him in His work in our day.

Notes

1. One verse earlier, John quotes Jesus as saying, "My kingdom is not of this world. If it were, my servants would fight to prevent my arrest by the Jews. But now my kingdom is from another place" (John 18:36). This does not negate the earthly reign of Messiah, but simply looks forward to what John describes in Revelation 21:1-4, following the thousand-year earthly reign, when the heavenly Jerusalem, the kingdom of heaven, joins the earthly Jerusalem so that God and humankind may dwell together once again.
2. Bill Johnson, *When Heaven Invades Earth* (Shippensburg, PA: Destiny Image, 2003), p. 57.
3. George Otis, Jr., *Informed Intercession* (Ventura, CA: Renew, 1999), pp. 18-23.
4. In that resurrection body, Jesus was able to walk through walls (see John 20:19) and disappear at will (see Luke 24:31), and He was able to eat (see John 21:12-13). Later He physically ascended to the Father (see Acts 1:9).
5. The word "Trinity" is not a biblical word, but it is often used to describe this one God who manifests Himself as Father, Son and Holy Spirit.
6. Paul E. Billheimer, *Destined for the Throne* (Minneapolis, MN: Bethany House Publishers, 1975), pp. 15-16. Italics in original.
7. Don Finto, *Your People Shall Be My People* (Ventura, CA: Regal Books, 2001), pp. 170-171,172.

WHAT DO MESSIANIC
JEWS BELIEVE?

*For in union with the Messiah, you are all children of God through this
trusting faithfulness; because as many of you as were immersed into the
Messiah have clothed yourselves with the Messiah, in whom there is
neither Jew nor Gentile, neither slave nor freeman, neither male nor
female; for in union with the Messiah Yeshua, you are all one.*

GALATIANS 3:26-28, *COMPLETE JEWISH BIBLE*

The early followers of Jesus were not "Christians." Not even
those who became believers on that first Shavuot (Pentecost)
after Jesus' resurrection. These were Jewish men and women
who had come to believe that Yeshua (Jesus) was the Promised
Messiah of Israel. On the day when 3,000 Jewish followers were
baptized into the Name of Yeshua, there was not the slightest
thought given to the founding of a new religion. Soon, with only
the men counted, the number rose to 5,000 (see Acts 2:41; 4:4).
Because of the persecution that followed, these early believers
began to be scattered, first to Judea and Samaria and then to distant Phoenicia, Cyprus and Antioch, where they spread the news
to their fellow Jews about the Messiah who had come (see 8:1;
11:19).

At first, these new believers continued to be a part of their
local synagogues. But the tensions increased, especially as uncircumcised Gentiles were added to the mix. For the next years,
there was a strange blend of Jews and Gentiles. Soon there were
more non-Jews who believed in the Jewish Messiah than there
were among the Jewish people. That fact began to produce an
even stranger set of circumstances. The tension between Rome
and Jerusalem ultimately ended with the destruction of
Jerusalem and the exile of all Jewish citizens. The Greek-
speaking world then began to call these new believers in the
Jewish Messiah Christians (see Acts 11:26). Although Jewish
Scriptures were their only Bible, non-Jewish believers distanced

themselves more and more from the Jewish roots of their faith. For centuries Israel had been the living witness of the only True God. Every slaughtered animal foreshadowed the coming of the Messiah, the Lamb of God. With the coming of Jesus, those Jewish feast days took on new meaning as they not only looked back to their historical beginnings but also now included the message of their fulfillment in Messiah Yeshua. Pesach was the anniversary of Jesus' execution. Shavuot became the memorial day for the outpouring of the *Ruach HaKodesh* (Holy Spirit). Yom Kippur (the Day of Atonement) was all about Jesus. But in the hearts of the Roman Christians, these holidays were not a part of their history, and with growing disdain for a nation that had rejected her Messiah, it soon seemed desirable for them to sever connections to the Jewish roots of the Christian faith. Obviously they could not reject Scripture, but it became easy to reinterpret promises to Israel as promises to the "new Israel," the Church, leaving only the curses for the nation that had birthed the Messiah.

The Council of Nicea formalized the separation. This was a "universal" gathering of the bishops of a totally Gentile Church. No Jewish bishop was invited, even though there was still a Jewish presence in that early fourth century. It was at this council that the date for celebrating the resurrection of Jesus, which had been changed from Passover to Easter by Pope Victor at the end of the second century, was made the official doctrine of the Church.[1] Soon the demand was made that the original host people abandon their heritage and begin to act more like Gentiles—eating pork, worshiping on Sunday, refraining from circumcising their sons and ceasing to celebrate the annual Jewish feasts.[2] The Church had disconnected from its roots (see Rom. 11:16-18), remaining separate until the rise of the Messianic Jewish movement in our day.

During the early days of the Puritans, some began to see that there would be a resurrection of the Jewish nation and the Jewish Church before the Lord's return—that the Church could only be completely healthy when Jew and Gentile united in Messiah. The *Geneva Bible* of 1560 comments on Romans 11:26 with these words: "He [Paul] sheweth that the time shall come that the whole nation of the Jews, though not every one particularly, shall be joined to the church of Christ."[3] Charles Spurgeon, the great British evangelist of the nineteenth century, was sure that "they shall be gathered in again."[4]

Although there were earlier attempts at starting a movement of Jewish synagogues of believers in Jesus,[5] it was not until the 1970s that these risen-from-the-dead Jewish congregations of believers began to form in the United States, in Israel, in the former Soviet Union and in many other nations.

WHAT IS THE DIFFERENCE BETWEEN A MESSIANIC CONGREGATION AND A CHURCH?

The two major associations of Jewish believers in the United States—the Union of Messianic Jewish Congregations (UMJC) and the Messianic Jewish Alliance of America (MJAA)—provide websites that clearly define the faith of the congregations associated with them.[6] Mainstream Jewish believers in Yeshua do not differ from Bible-believing Christians in their core faith in the divinity of Yeshua as fully God and fully man. Messianic believers, along with their Christian brothers and sisters, believe that through His death and shed blood, atonement for the sins of all humankind has been achieved. In addition, they accept the Bible as the only authoritative and infallible Word of God, consisting of both the Tanakh and the *B'rit Hadasha* (New Covenant) Scripture.

Congregations may differ as to the outworking of the Holy Spirit, yet they consistently affirm that it is only through the indwelling of the Spirit that believers are enabled to live godly lives. In the "Statement of Faith" of both the UMJC and the MJAA, faith is expressed in one God, eternally existent in three persons: Father, Son and Holy Spirit. Just as in traditional Jewish synagogues, so do Messianic congregations around the world join in reciting these words from the *Shema*, originally given by Moses and reaffirmed by Yeshua: "Hear, O Israel: The LORD our God, the LORD is one" (Deut. 6:4; quoted by Jesus in Mark 12:29).

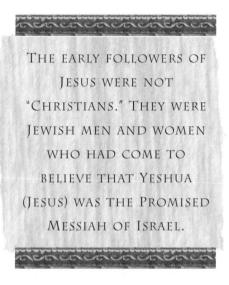

THE EARLY FOLLOWERS OF JESUS WERE NOT "CHRISTIANS." THEY WERE JEWISH MEN AND WOMEN WHO HAD COME TO BELIEVE THAT YESHUA (JESUS) WAS THE PROMISED MESSIAH OF ISRAEL.

Within the Messianic community there is wide variety in the way that Jewish identity is expressed, especially between the congregations in the Diaspora and those in the Land. *Tallitot* (prayer shawls) and *kippot* (yarmulkes) are much less often seen in the congregations within Israel than in their sister congregations in other countries. Those living in the Land have less need to prove that they are still Jewish.

On one of my frequent trips to Israel, I remember basking in the worship time of one rather large (for Israel), very vibrant congregation, when I suddenly realized that there was nothing visible that would identify this congregation as Jewish other than the people, the language in which we were worshiping and the place where we were meeting. There were no prayer shawls, no *menorah* (the seven-branched candle stand) and no reading from the Torah. Yet these were Jewish believers who had either gathered from the nations or had come to faith in Yeshua as Messiah while in the Land.

The celebration of biblical feasts is generally a "given" in any Messianic setting, though the manner in which the feasts are conducted may vary widely among groups, families or individuals. To those who live outside the Land, these biblical and cultural feasts are a way of maintaining Jewish identity as believers; to those inside the Land, the biblical festivals are often national holidays as well.

The covenant circumcision of sons on the eighth day and the coming-of-age celebrations for sons and daughters in the Bar Mitzvah and *Bat Mitzvah* rites, would also be a likely place of agreement across lines both in Israel and in the Diaspora.[7]

Rarely will a Messianic congregation meet on any day other than the biblical Sabbath (Saturday), with meetings either on *Erev Shabbat* (the eve of the Sabbath—Friday evening) or on the morning of the Sabbath. Here also one will find great variety in the gatherings; some are subdued in worship style and others are more expressive, with lively praise music and Davidic dance. Some will have considerable Jewish liturgy; others will have little or none. Sermons will more likely be taken from the Tanakh, with accompanying interpretations and selected passages from the B'rit Hadasha. Gatherings are often closed with the Aaronic Benediction, which is spoken or chanted in Hebrew (see Num. 6:24-26). One characteristic that will always be found in congregations outside Israel is their love and support for their brothers and sisters in the Land, for both believers and "not yet" believers.

Although there has been an amazing increase in Messianic congregations in the last 35 years, there are still probably more Jewish people who are a part of churches than who meet in specifically designated Jewish houses of worship. Some of this is due to the scarcity of Messianic congregations in all parts of the country; some, because the Jewish believers have come to faith through a church and have found a home among Christians; others, simply because they prefer the often larger, better-orchestrated congregations that are more prevalent in the Christian community. Among those who are members of churches, there will be even wider divergence in observance.

WHAT IS THE BEST WAY TO RELATE TO JEWISH BELIEVERS WHO ARE MEMBERS OF OUR CONGREGATIONS?

To help you understand the diversity of Jewish believers in Jesus, allow me to tell you two stories. One is of a brother who was reared in an Orthodox home in Israel, the grandson of an esteemed rabbi. I'll call him Oded. From earliest childhood, Oded wanted to be godly. He read the Torah regularly, studying both the sacred writings and the treasured words of the rabbis.

Oded had no desire to learn the ways of the world, which many of his contemporaries had learned. He wanted to know the God of his forefathers and to follow Him devoutly. Yet in the midst of his piety and commitment, Oded grew increasingly uneasy. Why had the Messiah never appeared? Why were there so many varieties of belief regarding the promised Anointed One?

One day while reading from the book of Zechariah, Oded was struck with the prophet's description of the King who would come: "righteous and having salvation, gentle and riding on a donkey, on a colt, the foal of a donkey" (9:9). *When will this King come?* Oded wondered. *The Word is clear. He will enter Jerusalem on a donkey. But I have never heard the rabbis speak of this. Why?*

Oded went to his rabbi, who told him that Zechariah was

not speaking of a literal donkey and that the prophet's words were to be understood symbolically—a spirit of righteousness would yet enter the city, bringing salvation to the nation.

But then one day Oded was given a copy of the B'rit Hadasha. He began to read about the One who came 2,000 years earlier and was received by many of His fellow countrymen as the Messiah. He read about miracles that this One supposedly worked—healing the sick and lame—just as Isaiah had predicted (see Isa. 35:5-6).

Then Oded came to Matthew 21. He read about Jesus' disciples finding a donkey and a colt and bringing them to Him. When Jesus actually mounted the donkey and rode into Jerusalem, Oded was stunned. *Here He is!* He thought. *This is that King!* He continued to read, realizing that his whole life would have to be reoriented to fit this revelation.

Oded had heard of a congregation of people who believed that Yeshua was Messiah. On the following Sabbath, he cautiously made his way to the congregation, wondering what he would find. *If there is a cross on the wall, I will not stay,* he thought. But as he entered the worship hall, he saw no cross.

Uncertain about what might occur during the worship service, Oded somewhat reluctantly sat down as the praise and worship began. But he noted little that resembled any synagogue he had ever known. After some time, the leaders of the congregation started toward the ark. Oded caught his breath, thinking, *That's where they keep the cross. It's hidden inside the ark.* But there was no cross. Only a Torah scroll that was carefully taken from its resting place, laid gently on a nearby table to find the *Parasha* (the Torah reading intended for each Sabbath). Oded was home. He later became a leader in that congregation, and he is now the spiritual leader of a newly established daughter congregation.

The second story, on the other hand, is about Yoni, who

completed his army duty, experienced the business world for a few years and left Israel, never expecting to return. Life was too difficult. He would find an easier path in another country. After a few months, he found himself working as a diving instructor in Cyprus. His roommate was a Christian, as was his boss. Both were praying that Yoni would come to know his Messiah.

One day Yoni's roommate invited him to go to church with him. Even though Yoni had no desire to go, he decided it might offer him some needed diversion, so he agreed. But he was totally unprepared for what lay ahead.

When he entered the building, the power of God fell over him. His legs began to tremble. He could not stand. Waves of love poured over him. *This is what drugs are supposed to be like,* Yoni thought, as his mind raced back through the years of searching for the panacea of life. *If I could find a drug like this, I would use it the rest of my life!*

At the conclusion of Yoni's first visit to a church, his friend gave him a copy of the New Testament. Yoni began to read: "the son of David, the son of Abraham. [H]e will save his people from their sins" (Matt. 1:1,21). *The book is Jewish. These are our prophets,* Yoni mused as he continued reading. *And this man is a son of David!*

On the following Sunday, Yoni was eager to go back to the church. He wanted that feeling again. But this time nothing happened. He continued to read his new Bible, becoming increasingly convinced that Jesus is the Promised World Redeemer. *But,* he thought, *this means that I will no longer be Jewish. I will be a Christian.* The thought did not repel him, since he had already decided that he would never return to Israel.

In a little town in the mountains of Cyprus, there is a Jewish family that runs a discipleship group. Yoni's roommate had heard of these "Christians" and suggested that he and Yoni pay them a visit on one of their weekend excursions. It was the *Chanukah* season, and the group was having some special meetings.

"These people are Jews!" Yoni muttered under his breath as he and his friend walked in and were greeted. "Let's don't stay! Let's get out of here!"

"No, they're Christians. I'm sure of it!" his friend insisted.

MAINSTREAM JEWISH BELIEVERS IN YESHUA DO NOT DIFFER FROM BIBLE-BELIEVING CHRISTIANS IN THEIR CORE FAITH IN THE DIVINITY OF YESHUA AS FULLY GOD AND FULLY MAN.

In the course of the evening, there were gifts to be exchanged, and these two newcomers were not to be left out. They, too, received gifts. When Yoni opened his package, he found a cross. Some of the Jewish believers, knowing that Yoni was Jewish but not knowing that he was a believer, assumed that he would be greatly offended. On the contrary, Yoni was overjoyed. He now had a visible expression of his newfound faith!

It was some time before Yoni understood that he had not forsaken his Jewishness by becoming a believer in the Jewish Messiah. He did not even have to call himself a Christian. Following his encounter with Messiah, Yoni spent several months at a discipleship training center with his believing bride, preparing for a life of service in the Body of Messiah Yeshua. Today, Yoni is being trained to spend the rest of his life proclaiming the message of his Messiah to all who will listen.

How does the church relate to these two very different personality types? Through careful sensitivity to the individual. This is a diverse people. Those of us from the nations often assume that the Jewish people will know more about the Old Testament than we, since it is "their" Book, yet some of Abraham's descendants know little or nothing about their own heritage. I remember challenging a young Jewish believer who was baptized in our home congregation in Nashville. He intended to bury his Jewishness in baptism, but I assured him that this was not something from which one can escape. He must learn how to serve his Messiah as one of His blood relatives, just as I am learning how to serve Him as I become a part of His family through adoption and spiritual heritage by faith.

I HAVE HEARD THAT MESSIANIC CONGREGATIONS USE ONLY THE OLD TESTAMENT IN THEIR GATHERINGS. IS THIS CORRECT?

No, it is not true that Messianic congregations use only the Old Testament in their gatherings. Every believer in Jesus as Messiah accepts the testimony of the apostles and their close friends, as recorded in what we call the New Testament. It is true, however, that emphasis is given to prophecy and to the revelation of Messiah as seen in the Hebrew Scriptures. One of my friends rightfully insists that if Jesus is absent in the Old Testament, then He is not the preincarnate Son of God.

Many Scriptures in the Tanakh indicate that the one God of the Shema is plural in nature, a plurality we later recognized as Father, Son and Holy Spirit. The very first verse of Genesis speaks of the plurality of God: the Hebrew word for the verb "created" is singular; the word for the noun "God"—*Elohim*—is plural. A singular verb with a plural noun. This same plurality is seen further in the Genesis story when God says, "Let *us* make man in *our* image, in *our* likeness" (Gen. 1:26, emphasis added). Isaiah articulates this plural nature of the one God when describing his own encounter with God: "I heard the voice of the Lord saying, 'Whom shall I send? And who will go for *us*?' " (Isa. 6:8, emphasis added). Who is this "us" of whom Isaiah speaks? Why does he quote God as saying "I" one moment and "us" the next if there is only one singular expression of Himself in all His being?

When Micah speaks of the One who will be "ruler over Israel," from Bethlehem Ephrathah, the prophet insists that His "origins are from of old, from ancient times" (Mic. 5:2). In other words, Messiah's birth was not His origin, just as the apostle John affirmed in the opening words of his Gospel. Jesus has existed "from ancient times."

In this regard the psalmist has a most interesting admonition to the nations of the world. Why do all the nations, the kings and the rulers "gather together against the LORD and against his Anointed One [Messiah]?" he asks (Ps. 2:1-2). Then he proceeds to tell the nations how this affects the Lord: "the One enthroned in heaven laughs; the Lord scoffs at them. Then he rebukes them in his anger and terrifies them in his wrath, saying, 'I have installed my King on Zion, my holy hill' " (vv. 4-6). Without question this psalm is about the King who is to come, this King whom we believers know as Yeshua.

But now listen to what God says in this prophetic messianic psalm: "He said to me, 'You are my Son; today I have become your Father. Ask of me, and I will make the nations your inheritance, the ends of the earth your possession. You will rule them with an iron scepter'" (Ps. 2:7-9). Very interesting! This King will rule the nations with a scepter, just as Jacob predicted regarding the Ruler who would come from the loins of Judah and just as John the apostle envisioned in his Revelation (see Gen. 49:10; Rev. 12:5). But this Ruler is also Son. The psalmist quotes God as saying, "Today I have become your Father," as though the relationship of these two Persons in the one God only assumed a Father-Son relationship at the Incarnation.

The idea of Jesus' being the Son of God is offensive to our rational mind, but this idea does not have its origin in the personal ministry of Jesus. Rather, its origin is the Hebrew Scripture. The psalmist's final admonition to these kings and rulers of the earth is this: "Serve the LORD with fear and rejoice with trembling. Kiss the Son, lest he be angry and you be destroyed in your way" (Ps. 2:11-12).

Not only do we sense the Presence of plurality in the one God in these Genesis and Psalm passages, but also we see the preincarnate Jesus in some of the Old Testament narratives. In Scripture, the word "LORD," in which all four letters are capitalized, is the English translation of the *YHVH,* the four Hebrew letters that refer to the Lord Himself, the Holy One. Many Jewish people will not even try to pronounce these letters; rather, they call Him *HaShem* (the Name), or *Adonai* (the Lord).

Carefully observe several well-known stories in which YHVH (the LORD), or Elohim (God), appears in human form and is worshiped as God. "The LORD appeared to Abraham" one day when he looked up and saw "three men standing nearby" (Gen. 18:1,2). Of the three, one was the Lord Himself. YHVH spoke to Abraham about the coming birth of Isaac and, later, about the approaching destruction of Sodom (see 18:10,16).

Moses encountered YHVH at the burning bush. "Take off your sandals, for the place where you are standing is holy ground," He said. Then He continued, "I am the God of your father, the God of Abraham, the God of Isaac and the God of Jacob" (Exod. 3:5-6). YHVH traveled with Israel the night they left Egypt, at times speaking to Moses and at other times looking down from the pillar of fire and the cloud (see 14:21-26).

Joshua met YHVH shortly after crossing the Jordan, when

He appeared first as a man with a drawn sword, who identified Himself as the "commander of the army of the LORD" (Josh. 5:14). Joshua worshiped Him as God. Had He been only an angel of God, He would not have allowed Joshua to worship Him, as John the apostle could testify when he bowed before an angel (see Rev. 19:9-10; 22:8-9).

Zechariah presents a very interesting revelation of Jesus. "I will pour out . . . a spirit of grace and supplication," says the Lord. "They [the people] will look on me, the one they have pierced" (12:10). God pours out His Spirit, but the same God who pours out His Spirit is the One they crucified.

Yes, Jesus is an active participant in the redemption of all of humanity, from the Garden until the final consummation of history. And yes, our Jewish brothers use the Hebrew Scriptures more often than most of our churches, but they accept the entire revelation of God, from Genesis to Revelation, as the inspired Word of God.

DID PAUL NOT SAY THAT CHRIST IS THE END OF THE LAW?

From the beginning to the end of Paul's Roman letter, as in all his letters to Gentiles, Paul speaks against those Judaizing teachers who were insisting that the Gentiles had to be keepers of the Law in order to receive the full blessings of the Messiah (Christ). The Torah does not make a person righteous, neither Jew nor Gentile, Paul declares. "No one will be declared righteous in his [God's] sight by observing the law; rather, through the law we become conscious of sin" (Rom. 3:20). "Law brings wrath" (4:15); only faith in the Messiah brings righteousness (see 3:21-22). "Do we, then, nullify the law by this faith? Not at all! Rather, we uphold the law" (v. 31). "I would not have known what coveting really was if the law had not said, 'Do not covet'," Paul goes on to say (7:7). "The law is holy, and the commandment is holy, righteous, and good" (v. 12). Paul's argument is that the Law fulfills its purpose when it points us to the One who redeems us by faith.

It is into this setting that Paul speaks these words: "Christ is the end of the law so that there may be righteousness for everyone who believes" (Rom. 10:4). The Law has not ceased to be, nor has it been abolished; rather, it has accomplished its purpose. Jesus made this quite clear by saying, "Do not think that I have come to abolish the Law or the Prophets; I have not come to abolish them but to fulfill them" (Matt. 5:17). The purpose of the Law in regard to righteousness—pointing to the One who was to come—is now completed.

A MESSIANIC JEW MUST LEARN HOW TO SERVE HIS MESSIAH AS ONE OF HIS BLOOD RELATIVES, JUST AS I AM LEARNING HOW TO SERVE HIM AS A PART OF HIS ADOPTED FAMILY.

The *New American Standard Bible* adds a marginal note to Romans 10:4, "Christ is the *end* of the law" (emphasis added), suggesting the word "goal" as another translation of the Greek word *telos,* the word translated as "end" in the verse.[8] The *New Living Translation* proposes this rendition of the verse: "Christ has accomplished the whole *purpose* of the law" (emphasis added). But David Stern's *Complete Jewish Bible* may give the best meaning of the verse: "For the *goal* at which the Torah aims is the Messiah, who offers righteousness to everyone who trusts" (emphasis added).

DO MESSIANIC BELIEVERS FIND ANY KIND OF ACCEPTANCE WITHIN THE LARGER JEWISH COMMUNITY?

Although for many centuries the Jewish community's generally accepted view has been that Jewish people who receive Jesus as Messiah are no longer to be considered Jewish, this appears to be gradually changing. I know one Orthodox rabbi who would affirm the position that Jewish believers in Jesus are no longer Jewish, while he, at the same time, enjoys an interesting fellowship with one of my sabra (native Israeli) friends, knowing that this man is a believer in Yeshua. Another rabbi whom I know rather well publicly explains to his people that a believer in Jesus forfeits his right to be Jewish as well as his right to membership in Jewish organizations, while this rabbi and I both know that some members of his congregation *do* believe that Jesus is the Messiah.

I have had occasion in recent months to enjoy close fellowship with two young Orthodox rabbis who believe in Jesus. One of these young men received his rabbinate ordination from a well-known yeshiva (school—in this case more like a seminary) even though he had acknowledged at the beginning of his studies that, though orthodox according to every acceptable definition, he believed that Yeshua is Messiah. He assumed that this would mean he would not be able to matriculate into the rabbinical Jewish studies, but he was pleasantly surprised when he received his acceptance letter a few days later.

While I was in Israel on another trip a few years ago, I was introduced to and fellowshipped with an Orthodox rabbi who had just recently come to faith, though he did not believe that the time had yet come for him to acknowledge his belief openly.

Two recent books written by rabbis—one by Reform Rabbi Dan Cohn-Sherbok and the other by Reconstructionist Rabbi Carol Harris-Shapiro—acknowledge Messianic Jews as Jewish. Cohn-Sherbok, in *Messianic Judaism,* concludes, "Messianic Judaism is no more inauthentic than other forms of contemporary Jewish life."[9] Harris-Shapiro, in *Messianic Judaism: A Rabbi's Journey Through Religious Change in America,* notes, "Under Messianic Jewish scrutiny, the American Jewish reasoning that accepts secular Jews but not Christian Jews as Jews, practicing Christian spouses of Jews as members of liberal synagogues but not Messianic Jews as members of liberal synagogues can appear fragile, fuzzy, even self-contradictory."[10] She goes on to suggest that this scenario may change in the next years, just as Reform Judaism has become an accepted branch of Judaism even though it was denied that acceptance when it first made its appearance in the nineteenth century.[11]

My Jewish colleague and friend Dan Juster says that in recent years no one has contributed more to the hard work of theological dialogue between Christians and Jews than the Jewish theologian Michael Wyschogrod.[12] This distinguished gentleman believes that "if the church acknowledges the abiding reality of Israel's corporeal election, it will naturally expect baptized Jews to maintain faithfully their Jewish identity. But if the church truly believes that it has superceded God's covenant with Israel, it will prohibit or discourage Jews from preserving their identity as Jews and members of the Jewish people."[13]

Wyschogrod is pushing the Church into a decision. If Israel is still Israel, then of course we will insist that Jews remain Jews, even if they believe in Yeshua. If, on the other hand, we believe that Israel is a thing of the past in God's eyes, then it follows that Jews lose their identity when they choose to believe in Jesus.

ARE GENTILES WELCOMED IN MESSIANIC CONGREGATIONS?

The intent of the Messianic movement is to encourage Jewish believers to maintain their Jewish identity as believers in Jesus rather than to assimilate into the Gentile Church, as was required of believers for most of the Church's history. Gentiles who become a part of the movement are expected to foster this identity so that their presence does not diminish that congregation's call to the larger Jewish community.

The Union of Messianic Jewish Congregations requires at least 10 Jewish members before a congregation can be considered for membership in the Union. Articulating such a requirement acknowledges that there are many Gentiles who become a part of the Messianic congregations. The Messianic Jewish Alliance of America recognizes in its statement of faith that "Gentiles who place their faith in *Yeshua* are 'grafted into' the Jewish olive tree of faith (Rom. 11:17-25), becoming spiritual sons and daughters of Abraham (Gal. 3:28-19)."[14]

Some of us believe that as the Church becomes more and more aware of its Jewish heritage, she will begin to recognize the biblical calendar and the biblical feasts. When this occurs, we will have a multiplicity of Messianic Jewish congregations that each have a healthy contingent of Gentile covenant partners, as well as "Messianic Gentile" congregations in which our Jewish brothers and sisters find a more responsive home. For this to happen, the Church must come to embrace her Jewish roots.

Notes

1. Passover is observed on the same day of each year on the lunar/biblical/Jewish calendar—the 14th day of the first month (Nisan). At the Council of Nicea, the date for the Western Church's celebration of the Jesus' resurrection was fixed to follow the first full moon after the vernal equinox (March 21), the first official calendar day of Spring. In some years, these two dates are quite close—only a few days apart. In other years, they can be weeks apart. The name "Easter" is derived from the goddess of Spring and the dawn, Ostara (or Eastre). *The New Schaff-Herzog Encyclopedia of Religious Knowledge* (Grand Rapids, MI: Baker Book House, 1953), s.v. "Passover/ Easter."

2. Circumcision was a sign of the covenant of God on their nation, and the annual Jewish feasts had found their fulfillment in the Messiah.

3. *Geneva Bible,* quoted in Iain H. Murray, *The Puritan Hope: Revival and the Interpretation of Prophecy* (Carlisle, PA: The Banner of Truth Trust, 1971, reprinted in 1998), p. 72.

4. Charles H. Spurgeon, *Metropolitan Tabernacle Pulpit* series of sermons, vol. 17, pp. 703, quoted in Murray, *The Puritan Hope: Revival and the Interpretation of Prophecy,* p. 256.

5. Kai Kjaer-Hansen, in his book *The Herzl of Jewish Christianity: Joseph Rabinowitz and the Messianic Movement* (Grand Rapids, MI: Wm. B. Eerdmans Publishing Co., 1995), chronicles a thriving, late nineteenth-century synagogue in Kishinev, Moldova, which unfortunately did not survive into the twentieth century.

6. The website for the Union of Messianic Jewish Congregations is www.umjc.org; for Messianic Jewish Alliance of America, it is www.mjaa.org.

7. The Bat Mitzvah celebration, in which daughters are received as "daughters of the law," is a modern addition to Jewish tradition, coming more from the Reform Jewish movements, but it is generally received in the Messianic movement.

8. *New American Standard Bible, Reference Edition.* © 1960, 1962, 1971, 1973 by the Lockman Foundation, note to Romans 10:4.

9. Dan Cohn-Sherbok, *Messianic Judaism* (New York: Cassell, 2000), p. 213.

10. Carol Harris-Shapiro, *Messianic Judaism: A Rabbi's Journey Through Religious Change in America* (Boston: Beacon Press, 1999), p. 17.

11. Ibid., p. 170.

12. Michael Wyschogrod, one of the leading orthodox theologians alive today, is Professor of Systematic Theology at Wesley Theological Seminary in Washington, DC.

13. Michael Wyschogrod, quoted in R. Kendall Soulen, *The God of Israel and Christian Theology* (Minneapolis, MN: Fortress Press, 1996), p. 11.

14. Messianic Jewish Alliance of America, "MJAA Statement of Faith," 2004. http://mjaa.org/StatementOfFaith.html#israel (accessed July 26, 2005).

WHY SHOULD THE CHURCH EMBRACE HER JEWISH ROOTS?

He redeemed us in order that the blessing given to Abraham
might come to the Gentiles through Christ Jesus.

"If the root is holy, so are the branches," Paul told the Roman Christians (Rom. 11:16). The root of the "Christian" faith is the family of Abraham through Isaac and Israel. For 20 centuries this root nation has not accepted her Messiah,[1] but as the Jewish people are gradually accepting the Messiah, so the Church is little by little grasping what it means to be "fellow citizens" with Israel (Eph. 2:19).

PAUL SPEAKS OF THE GRAFTING OF THE GENTILES IN TO THE OLIVE ROOT OF ISRAEL IN ROMANS 11:17. WHAT IS GRAFTING? HOW IS IT DONE? EXACTLY TO WHAT IS PAUL REFERRING?

These excellent questions were posed by a student at the International House of Prayer in Kansas City at our Israel Mandate Conference in March 2004. Until then, it had never occurred to me that, since the United States is no longer a nation of farmers and gardeners, most of us have never seen a branch from one tree grafted in to another tree.

In Romans 11, Paul calls Israel "a cultivated olive tree" (v. 24). God picked her from the nations (Ur of the Chaldeans) and began to train and cultivate her. He pruned and cared for her, gave her the Law, spoke to her through the prophets and disciplined her for 1,500 years prior to the coming of the Redeemer. Because of the words of the prophets, Israel was expecting the Messiah.

The Gentiles, on the other hand, had no such expectation. They—the surrounding nations—were wild and had little or no revelation of the God of creation. They were unaware of the covenant made with Abraham and the patriarchs; they had not heard the prophetic words; they had not experienced the same pruning and discipline from the Lord. Today, through the mercies of God, their wild branches are being grafted in to this Abrahamic root system.

I grew up on a West Texas farm where there was not an abundance of either water or fruit trees. So sometimes, to obtain a variety of fruit, my family would find a very healthy fruit tree and graft branches from another, less vigorous tree to this "parent" tree. Branches from different kinds of apple trees can be grafted in to one tree. Pear and apple branches can be grafted into quince roots. Plum branches can be grafted in to peach trees. The interesting thing about grafting is that, although the water and nutrient supply come from the parent tree, the fruit is the original fruit with finer texture, shape and flavor because of its better nutrient supply. It contains the sap from the tree to which it is rooted; the health of the fruit is dependent on the health of the root system. That is exactly Paul's point. The Church, separated from her Jewishness (her Jewish roots), can never know full health.

What an apt description of the nations being united with Israel! Many of Israel's branches were, according to Paul (see Rom. 11:17), temporarily cut off from their own olive root, while we, the nations, were grafted in to their root system. We receive the "sap" (the life force, the spiritual nutrients) from their root structure (the Holy Spirit, the promises, the heritage). This does not change who we are, but it enables us to be all that we are intended to be.

This is God's plan for the nations. The nation God called through Abraham, Isaac and Israel possesses the only root system that will bring forth a life that lasts for all eternity. "Salvation [eternal health] is from the Jews," Jesus told the Samaritan woman (John 4:22). The saved of all the nations have been graft-ed in to one tree.

As "wild olive branches" from Uganda and Brazil and Tonga and China are grafted in to Israel's cultivated tree, they draw on the sap of their Jewish roots, but they do not look Jewish. They look like "healthy" Ugandans and Brazilians and Tongans and Chinese, in whose veins flows Jewish sap, even Jewish blood—Jesus' blood.

Having been grafted in, we do not all begin to put on a yarmulke for prayer or wrap a Jewish prayer shawl around our shoulders. We do not all begin to speak Hebrew nor do we all circumcise our sons, as the apostles made clear through the decisions of the council of apostles and elders in Jerusalem (see Acts 15). But we do receive the revelation given to the Jews. We are deeply affected by their feasts—all of which speak of our Savior. We are led to the Messiah through their Law (see Gal. 3:24). We accept their prophets and apostles as our own, and even become citizens of Israel (see Eph. 2:12). We are grafted in to their tree.

WHEN PAUL TELLS THE ROMANS THAT "NOT ALL WHO ARE DESCENDED FROM ISRAEL ARE ISRAEL" (9:6), IS HE SAYING THAT THE JEWISH PEOPLE WHO HAVE REJECTED THEIR MESSIAH ARE NO LONGER JEWS?

The passage in question is from Paul's letter to the predominant-ly non-Jewish Roman Church, a letter in which he lays out not only a clear theology of the completed work of Jesus at the cross but also instructions for how Jew and Gentile are to relate, since they have received the fulfillment of the promise God gave through Abraham.

In the first two chapters of his Roman letter, Paul speaks of his own special assignment "to call people from among all the Gentiles to the obedience that comes from faith" (1:5), but he reminds his non-Jewish hearers that the gospel is "first for the Jew, then for the Gentile" (v. 16) and that "trouble and distress," as well as "glory, honor and peace," will come "first for the Jew, then for the Gentile" (2:9-10).

In the ensuing chapters, Paul presents a precise theology on the inability of righteousness to be attained through human effort, through obedience to any law—even the Mosaic Law—declaring, "Now God's way of putting people right with himself has been revealed. It has nothing to do with law, even though the Law of Moses and the prophets gave their witness to it" (3:21, *TEV*).

After he clearly makes his point that our eternal salvation and our sanctification (becoming godly, holy people) rest exclusively in the completed work of Jesus and that His Holy Spirit now operates within us to complete His work, Paul returns to the relationship of Jew and non-Jew and asks, "Did God reject his people?" He responds forthrightly, "By no means!" (11:1). God has hardened their hearts and closed their eyes for a season, according to His divine purposes (see v. 8, which refers to Isa. 6:9-10), so that at this present moment, only a remnant have accepted their Messiah (see v. 5). But they have not stumbled beyond recovery (see v. 11); they will yet come to their fullness (see v. 12). They will experience acceptance (see v. 15), and they will be "grafted into their own olive tree" (v. 24), where all Israel will ultimately be saved (see v. 26).

It is in the midst of this discussion that the passage in question is spoken; therefore, it must be interpreted in light of the entire context. Romans 9:6-8 reads,

> Not all who are descended from Israel are Israel. Nor because they are his descendants are they all Abraham's

children. On the contrary, "It is through Isaac that your off-spring will be reckoned." In other words, it is not the natural children who are God's children, but it is the children of the promise who are regarded as Abraham's offspring.

What then can Paul mean? In chapters 3 through 8, he speaks forcefully about the "family of faith." Even Abraham was accounted righteous on the basis of faith, not on the basis of works. Only the descendants of Abraham who have the faith of Abraham have fully entered into the promise of Abraham. They are not the Israel that God intended. They have yet to acknowledge the Messiah.

On the other hand, we non-Jews who have the faith of Abraham have been grafted in to the family and look forward to the time when the rest of our "adoptive" family will come into the fullness of the promise that has been so graciously granted to us all.

Just as those members of my own blood family who have not come into the covenant are still my family, so also are my new Jewish family members who have not yet come to faith in Yeshua as their Messiah. My new family does not even recognize me as one of them. I am simply in on a mystery that they do not yet comprehend.

DOES PAUL NOT MAKE IT VERY CLEAR THAT IN JESUS, RACE IS NO LONGER AN ISSUE—THAT WE ARE ALL ONE IN HIM?

The Jewish apostle Paul was specifically called by God to go to the Gentiles (see Acts 9:15; Rom. 11:13; 15:15-16; Gal. 1:16; 2:7-8). Most of his letters were addressed to a predominantly Gentile readership. In these letters, especially in the letter to the Galatians, he defines the relationship that Jews and Gentiles have with each other.

To the Romans, Paul points out that, though we are all now grafted in to the same tree, there are definite distinctions and benefits to be found in a Jewish heritage. "What advantage, then, is there in being a Jew, or what value is there in circumcision?" he asks, before answering his own question. "Much in every way! First of all, they have been entrusted with the very words of God" (3:1,2).

Even though Paul's ministry was primarily to the Gentiles, he still went to the Jewish synagogues when first entering a new city. This was in keeping with the criteria he lays down to the Romans: that the gospel was to be preached first to the Jew and then to the Gentiles (see 1:16). Although Paul himself was a Torah-observing, feast-celebrating, Sabbath-keeping Jew who required his Jewish companions to be circumcised, he warns in Galatians against those who would insist on circumcision for non-Jews. This was the controversy that brought about the Acts 15 Jerusalem council.

Paul summarizes by saying that we are "all sons of God through faith in Christ Jesus. . . . There is neither Jew nor Greek, slave nor free, male nor female, for you are all one in Christ Jesus" (Gal. 3:26,28). Just as male and female do not surrender their gender when they become one in marriage, neither do Jews surrender their Jewishness, nor Gentiles their Gentileness, when they come together as one in Messiah.

IT SEEMS LIKE SOME WHO CONNECT WITH THE JEWISH ROOTS OF THEIR FAITH GO OFF THE DEEP END AND BEGIN TO DO SUCH THINGS AS DEMAND THAT GENTILES CHANGE THEIR MEETING DAY FROM SUNDAY TO THE SABBATH. IS THAT BIBLICAL?

The Western world is driving itself insane, spending millions on psychiatrists and drugs, often because of the forgotten commandment. We believers accept without question nine of the Ten Commandments as valid for our time. We understand the nine commandments to be included in the two commandments given to us by the Lord, the commandments on which "all the Law and the Prophets hang": loving God with all our hearts, souls and minds, and loving our neighbors as ourselves (see Matt. 22:37-40). Yet it may seldom occur to some people that there is a missing ingredient—the command to rest—that allows us to love both God and man. By keeping the Sabbath holy (see Exod. 20:8), we are reminded each week that God is not a God who enslaves, but that He is a God of love, who will take care of us if we will honor His Word.

The Jerusalem council made it clear that Gentiles were not to be held to a strict observance of the Mosaic Law, as had been required of the Jewish brothers (see Acts 15:1-29). In Romans and Galatians, we learn from Paul that the Law was never intended to bring righteousness (see Rom. 3:20; Gal. 3:11). It was intended to point to the One who would give us righteousness by faith. We have no merit in God's sight because of our acts of obedience. We do draw closer to Him and become more like Him as we obey Him, but none of that saves us. We are saved—accepted as righteous—when we receive by faith the finished work of Jesus on the cross.

Sabbath observance is, therefore, not a legal matter; but as we better understand God's intentions, it becomes a blessing. God did not demand that we worship on a specific day; instead, in His goodness, He desires that we learn to rest. We are no longer slaves. He will provide for us if we work six days and set aside a day of rest on the seventh—a scenario that He Himself modeled for us at the Creation.

More than that, God will work on our behalf as we delight in the Sabbath and rest in Him:

"If you keep your feet from breaking the Sabbath and from doing as you please on my holy day, if you call the Sabbath a delight and the LORD'S holy day honorable, and if you honor it by not going your own way and not doing as you please or speaking idle words, then you will find your joy in the LORD, and I will cause you to ride on the heights of the land and to feast on the inheritance of your father Jacob." The mouth of the LORD has spoken (Isa. 58:13-14).

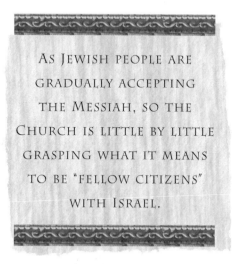

AS JEWISH PEOPLE ARE GRADUALLY ACCEPTING THE MESSIAH, SO THE CHURCH IS LITTLE BY LITTLE GRASPING WHAT IT MEANS TO BE "FELLOW CITIZENS" WITH ISRAEL.

Jesus observed the Sabbath differently from his contemporaries. When confronted, He said, "The Sabbath was made for man, not man for the Sabbath" (Mark 2:27). This is a Jesus-originated principle that must underlie all Sabbath observance. The kind of Sabbath rest to which Jesus and the prophets are speaking is a blessing, not a burden, to man.

I challenge you to set aside God's seventh day for rest. Do no work. Turn off the entertainment channels or other communication channels that so often consume us. Prepare enough "manna" on the other six days so that all can rest (see Exod. 16:25-26). Begin to settle down at sunset on the previous evening. (If you read Genesis 1 again, you will notice that God's days begin in the evening.) Remember the Lord. Draw the family together and enjoy each other. If, for some reason, it is not possible for you to make the

Sabbath your day of rest, then find another day. Obey, in principle at least, the fourth commandment.

My friend Rauf Mattin, an Iranian-born Christian, bought the pizza parlor down the street from our house. For the first few months, Rauf kept the store open seven days a week simply because it had always been kept open, but Rauf understood God's Sabbath intention to give His people rest. Rauf began closing the store each Sunday (that was his understanding of Sabbath rest). The Lord met Rauf at his place of faith—and the profits increased.

WHAT IS THE MEANING OF PAUL'S ADMONITION TO THE COLOSSIANS NOT TO ALLOW ANYONE TO JUDGE THEM ON THE BASIS OF WHAT THEY ATE OR DRANK OR HOW THEY OBSERVED RELIGIOUS HOLIDAYS?

Paul constantly warns believers not to depend on their own righteousness as a means of earning their salvation, nor to take pride in their spiritual growth. These are gifts from God. We are never to get so caught up in observances that we neglect the One from whom all good gifts come. "You have been given fullness in Christ," Paul wants the Colossians to know. "God made you alive with Christ. He forgave us all our sins" (2:10,13). Paul's message is this: "Don't allow someone to bring you back under a legal system as if it could impart life."

Having made his point, Paul further advises, "Do not let anyone judge you by what you eat or drink, or with regard to a religious festival, a New Moon celebration or a Sabbath day. These are a shadow of the things that were to come; the reality, however, is found in Christ" (2:16-17). This works out in our lives—as it did for the Colossians—in two ways: (1) We are not to allow fellow believers to place legalistic burdens on us, as if there were spiritual merit in the observances themselves; (2) We are also not to allow nonbelieving neighbors and friends to keep us from the very things that would be a blessing. Let all things be done to the glory of God!

SOME OF MY FRIENDS SAY THAT WE GENTILES ARE ALL A PART OF EPHRAIM, THE LOST TRIBES OF ISRAEL. WHERE DO THEY GET THIS UNDERSTANDING? IS THERE ANY VALIDITY TO IT?

At King Solomon's death, the kingdom of Israel was divided into two kingdoms. King David's lineage through his son Rehoboam retained only the tribes of Judah and Benjamin in the South. The 10 northern tribes named Jeroboam as their king, and they began to be known as the kingdom of Israel. This northern kingdom is often referred to in prophecy by the name of its principal tribe, Ephraim. The northern kingdom fell in 722 B.C., and many of its citizens were taken as captives to the conquering Assyria. One hundred years later, when King Josiah reigned over the southern kingdom, he found the Book of the Law, cleansed the Temple, collected money "from the people of Manasseh, Ephraim, and the entire remnant of Israel" (2 Chron. 34:9) and then invited "all Judah and Israel" to the grandest Passover celebration since the days of the prophet Samuel (see 35:18).

Out of this story has grown a theory that we, the Gentiles who have come to faith in Yeshua, are the rediscovered blood descendants of tribes that were dispersed to the nations through the Assyrian conquest. This hypothesis grows out of a certain translation of the Hebrew word *goyim* in Genesis 48:19, where Jacob (Israel) promises to Ephraim that his descendants shall become a group of nations. The assumption is that "a group of nations" (goyim) can only refer to nations other than Israel, but this ignores a passage like Exodus 19:6, where the Lord promises Israel that she is to be "a holy nation" (*goy*) before Him.

The Ephraimite movement blurs the lines of the restoration of the children of Israel to the Land, assuming a lineage that is without proof. It further causes Gentiles to believe that there is special validation in being a part of the 10 tribes, even though Paul is constantly assuring his fellow believers among the Gentiles that "[we] are all one in Christ Jesus" (Gal. 3:28). Furthermore, if all of us who believe in Jesus are Israel, as the theory purports, then who are the Gentiles, who are referred to throughout the Bible?

Much speculation has arisen over the fate of the northern tribes, as well as all those who have been dispersed to the nations. One of my friends, while traveling in the Republic of Georgia, visited a Jewish community that traces its lineage back 2,600 years ago to the time of the Assyrian exile. There have been Jewish communities in Africa, China, India and other countries throughout the world that believe they are part of that scattered community. Latin America is filled with Sephardic Jewish names, which most likely have come from Jewish people who left Spain and Portugal in the fifteenth century and whose descendants are now "hidden" among the nations. Eastern Europe's communism often eradicated the heritage of the Jewish people, but it is now slowly being restored.

It was never God's intention to make all of us blood descendants of Abraham; but rather, through Abraham, God chose to bless all the families of the earth. That promise to our spiritual father was articulated to Israel throughout her history. She was to be a light to the nations, bringing salvation to the ends of the earth.

Recently I received a letter from a brother who chastised me for referring to myself as a Gentile, since I have become a part of Israel by faith. True, I am grafted in, but I am a wild olive root (Gentile) that has been grafted in to the original cultivated olive tree (Israel). We non-Jews need not have an identity crisis. We are citizens of Israel by faith. We have no need to call ourselves Jewish. This was true in the New Covenant era, and it remains true today.

Is the Church supposed to be celebrating the Jewish feasts?

I love to go out under the night skies during a full moon. I always smile as I look up at the pale golden orb. God throws three big parties a year: Pesach (Passover), Shavuot (Pentecost) and Sukkot (Feast of Tabernacles). Pesach and Shavuot, and generally also Sukkot, arrive when the moon is at its brightest. God wanted to make sure that there was sufficient light overhead for the celebrations. If I happen to be looking at the moon during the lunar month of *Adar*, then I think, *That's right! It's only another month until Passover.* If my night vision is in the month of *Elul*, then I know that the next full moon will be on the fifteenth of the lunar month *Tishri*, the beginning of the Feast of Tabernacles.

Although the Gentiles were not specifically instructed regarding the biblical feasts, they were, from the beginnings of the Church, reading from the Hebrew Bible (there was not yet a collection of writings from the apostles). They were, therefore, aware of the feasts and their New Covenant meaning; and according to 1 Corinthians 5:7-8, they celebrated these festivals along with their Jewish brothers and sisters. That the Corinthian believers recognized the biblical (Jewish) calendar is also seen in Paul's reference to Jesus' resurrection as the "firstfruits" of many others who would follow (1 Cor. 15:20).

The prophet Zechariah indicates that during the future reign of Messiah, all the nations will be represented at the annual Feast of Tabernacles celebration in Jerusalem in order to assure that they will have adequate rainfall in the following year (see Zech. 14:16-19). The prophet speaks further of the plague that will be inflicted on the nations that do not go up to celebrate the Feast (see v. 18). The multiple thousands of Christians from the nations who today travel to Jerusalem to celebrate the Feast each year are a symbolic international prophetic statement to the world that Zechariah's words will one day find total fulfillment.

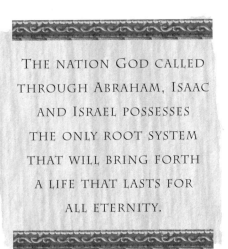

THE NATION GOD CALLED THROUGH ABRAHAM, ISAAC AND ISRAEL POSSESSES THE ONLY ROOT SYSTEM THAT WILL BRING FORTH A LIFE THAT LASTS FOR ALL ETERNITY.

These biblical feasts have great significance for all believers. Jesus was crucified at Pesach and was raised on the Feast of Firstfruits. Just as the Law of Moses was given at the first Shavuot, 50 days after Israel's Passover in Egypt, so the "law of the Spirit of life" in Messiah Jesus (Rom. 8:2) was given at another Shavuot—50 days after the death of our Passover Lamb, Jesus (see Acts 2:1-4). Rosh Hashanah, meaning "the head of the year," introduces the fall feasts, including Sukkot, also called the Feast of Trumpets. Sukkot is held at the closing harvest and is reminiscent of Paul's reference to the last trumpet sound that beckons God's people at the harvest (see 1 Cor. 15:52; 1 Thess. 4:16) and of Jesus' mention of the trumpet call of God when the elect will be gathered "from one end of the heavens to the other" (Matt. 24:31).

Since the Early Church celebrated the biblical feasts as fulfilled in Messiah Jesus and the end-time Church will still be celebrating them, and since these feasts are still meaningful proclamations of the good news about Jesus, it would seem natural for us Gentiles to pay more attention even now to the biblical calendar and the biblical feasts.

I hear people say that we should have a Hebrew mind-set rather than a Greek mind-set. What do they mean?

Let me answer your question by telling you of a conversation I had with a young man who "shadowed" me for one year in a mentoring relationship. On our first day, I told him, "If we are going to live together for a year and if you are to learn from me, I am going to live out loud with you. When I pray, I will pray aloud. I will process life aloud with you. You will see my flaws as well as experience my strengths. You will come to know how I deal with anger, stress, disappointments and temptation; situations where I am misunderstood or accused, as well as times when I am honored, held in esteem or walking in great joy."

During our first week, we attended a conference. The first night's speaker was very disappointing. I was ready to leave long before the conclusion of the program. "Now, did that message challenge you?" I asked my young friend on our way out of the building. "You understand that we are not to promote ourselves as the world's judges, but you also need to know that this is not the kind of preaching to which you want to aspire. That brother is a fine brother, but his message did not come across to me with any measure of anointing."

We stayed at the conference and attended many more meetings. We "thought out loud" together and were challenged again and again, both by the fellowship and by other messages. We processed life with each other. How could we have done this if both of us had remained silent or if I had done all the talking and he had not been allowed to share? This personal, involved, costly mentoring process is part of what is meant by "a Hebrew mind-set."

The Greek mind-set, when applied to an educational system, stresses relaying information from mind to mind. It is assumed that if our belief systems and knowledge are correct, we will become productive members of society. In an educational system based on the Greek worldview, professionals, who may never have entered fully into the life of the society, train other professionals. The teacher imparts knowledge to a room full of students, the character of the teacher and the students being of little importance. Revelations made known by the Western press in recent years are adequate evidence of the impact that a Greek educational system ultimately has on society. Who cares whether leaders are moral or honest or faithful to their covenants as long as we all have adequate food on the table and the luxuries to which we have become accustomed?

As I already explained while describing my relationship with my yearlong shadow, the Hebrew style of producing disciples is learning through mentoring and apprenticeships. The teacher is one whose life the student wishes to emulate—leadership by personal example, living together rather than having only relatively superficial encounters in a classroom. This method tends to promote transparency of life between the teacher and the student as they fellowship in a continual learning process that affects both of them. It has to do with love and acceptance and forgiveness. It produces character. Jesus' mentoring of his disciples is our finest example of the Hebrew style. The disciples learned as they lived in His presence. They listened, but they also observed His actions and attitudes. Only a life lived in such openness has power to transform and impart life to another.

———————

By this time you may be a bit overwhelmed. You may be thinking, *Is all that I have read in this book true? If so, how am I to respond?* First, let me encourage you once again not to accept what I have written just because it's in a book. Read the Word for yourself. Check out what I've written. Listen for God to speak to you. And then, stay with me just a little longer and let's think about this together.

Note

1. Many individual Jewish people have come to faith through the centuries, but never has the nation of Israel as a whole embraced Yeshua as Messiah, as Paul predicts will happen (see Rom. 11:26).

HOW SHOULD CHRISTIANS
RESPOND?

If the Gentiles have shared in the Jews' spiritual blessings, they owe it to the Jews to share with them their material blessings.

ROMANS 15:27

As we have opportunity, let us do good to all people, especially to those who belong to the family of believers.

GALATIANS 6:10

Although Jews and Gentiles are now one in the Messiah, we Gentiles still owe our heritage to our Jewish brothers and sisters. They are our older brothers of faith who will forever retain a place of honor in the family. "They have been entrusted with the very words of God," the apostle Paul tells us (Rom. 3:2), and they have meticulously and carefully handed down that word to each succeeding generation. We non-Jewish believers in this Jewish Messiah will do well to ponder what our response to the Jewish community is to be.

HOW CAN CHRISTIANS RELATE TO THE JEWISH COMMUNITY AT LARGE AND STILL SUPPORT THEIR MESSIANIC JEWISH BROTHERS AND SISTERS?

I'm glad you asked! My love for Israel and the Jewish people grew as I studied Scripture and the Lord revealed more and more of His love for His covenant people. But this love was also greatly influenced by the early Messianic Jewish movement and by some of my flock who were Jewish. Having once entered this door of love, and in recognition of my status as a grafted-in son of Israel, I now embrace the entire family of Israel as a part of myself. Nonetheless, it has not always been easy to know how to navigate that love, because the Jewish community at large does not appreciate my belief that Jesus is the Messiah of both Jews and non-Jews.

A few years ago, I returned to Nashville from a Toward Jerusalem Council II[1] meeting. I was delighted by the rich time of fellowship that I had enjoyed with these Jewish and non-Jewish believers in Jesus, and I wanted the whole world to know about it! I wanted to share with others the experience of Jews and Gentiles coming together in understanding and celebration of the love and grace of God. Consequently, I spent the entire sermon time the next week telling about the amazing rise of the Messianic Jewish community.

ALTHOUGH JEWS AND GENTILES ARE NOW ONE IN THE MESSIAH, WE GENTILES STILL OWE OUR HERITAGE TO OUR JEWISH BROTHERS AND SISTERS.

One of the sisters of my congregation was deeply moved by the message. She thought the sermon tape would be perfect to give to a Jewish neighbor with whom she had had many discussions. On her way out of the assembly that morning, she picked up a cassette and gave it to her neighbor. He, in turn, passed it on to his rabbi, who happened to be a friend of mine.

A few days later I received a phone call. "Don," said my rabbi friend, "I am not pleased with the message that you brought to your church. This is not the way to develop friendship in the Jewish community."

"Michael," I replied, "surely this is not new to you. You know what I believe. Can't we be friends even if we do not agree?"

"No," he retorted, "not if you are hoping that I will change!"

"Have I ever coerced you?" I replied. "Of course, I wish you believed what I believe. Do you not wish that I believed what you believe? Does the difference have to harm our friendship?"

Our friendship was not to be. I had often visited my friend's synagogue and had even been invited to his son's Bar Mitzvah. I had enjoyed a Passover seder with his congregation and had participated in many congenial discussions, both public and private. But my message on the Messianic Jewish people, delivered to my own flock, had greatly disturbed him—so much so that he made his offense public. A few weeks later, I awakened to these front-page headlines in our daily Nashville newspaper: "Rabbi Offended by Pastor's Remarks."[2] The next few weeks were filled with talk shows and newscasts that featured the "controversy." It was not an easy time for me. The very people that I had come to love so much felt that I had betrayed them!

No, this is not a simple path that we have chosen—loving the entire Jewish community while maintaining a deep fellowship with those of Jewish heritage who have come to believe that Jesus is the Messiah—but it is one we are determined to walk.

Being one who seeks to advocate for Jewish believers in Jesus without offending those Jewish brothers who disagree with me can sometimes place me in a difficult position. A few years ago, I was asked to lead one of the prayers at the annual Tennessee Governor's Prayer Breakfast. When I arrived and was ushered to my position on the platform, I found myself seated next to another of Nashville's rabbis, who was to have the Old Testament reading. We engaged in cordial conversation, and then I was called upon for the prayer. When I was about to close, I articulated, slowly and carefully, "I bring this to You in the Name of Jesus. Amen."

When I sat down, the rabbi commented, "I appreciate the way you said that."

I smiled. "I do not expect you to pray in the Name of Jesus, but I do—I have to."

That reminds me of another conversation I had with a nationally known rabbi who works as a liaison to the Christian community out of one of Israel's consulates. I told him of my dilemma—that I love the Jewish people, but I cannot compromise my own faith. I was startled by his response. "I tell my Christian friends," he said, "that the day they quit praying in the Name of Jesus is the day I no longer want to be around them."

It took me a moment to catch the significance of his remark. What he was really saying was this: "The day you compromise your convictions in order to be my friend, I would no longer trust you. I would wonder what else you would compromise. What about your love for me and my people? Would you one day sacrifice us in order to please someone else?"

It was not the Bible-believing Church of Austria and Germany that turned her back on the Jewish people in the days of the Nazi reign of terror. It was, rather, the compromising Church that no longer believed the Book—that had long before begun shelving her convictions. It will not be the Bible-believing Church that will turn her back on the Jewish people in the future. It will be that part of the "Church" that has ceased believing the Book.

My conversations with these rabbis have helped me shape future meetings between Christians and Jews. When asked to address such a group, I usually begin by stepping into a role similar to that of the prophet Daniel, who in prayer took upon himself the sins of his people—of kings long dead and of those who lived many miles away. "We have sinned," Daniel prayed. "We have been wicked and have rebelled. . . . We have not listened to your servants the prophets, who spoke in your name to our kings, our princes and our fathers, and to all the people of the land" (9:5-6). Daniel had not sinned, but he was willing to take the sins of others upon himself as an act of intercession.

Similarly, when I address meetings of Jews and Christians, I follow Daniel's lead by confessing the atrocities of the past against the Jewish communities; then I thank my Jewish friends for daring to attend a gathering of Christians. I am not certain that I would be able to come to such a gathering, had I been reared as they—having heard the centuries-long horror stories and accusations that the Church leveled against the Jewish people. I speak candidly of our differences, but I pledge to them that millions of us have entered a covenant similar to the one between Ruth and Naomi: "Your people [are now] my people and your God my God. Where you die I will die, and there I will be buried. May the LORD deal with me, be it ever so severely, if anything but death separates you and me" (Ruth 1:16-17). I tell them about my conversations with the rabbi at the prayer breakfast and with the rabbi from the Consul General's office, and yes, I tell them that I pray in Jesus' Name. But I also tell them that even in disagreement, my commitment is not diminished.

Those of us making such a commitment will soon have ample opportunity to prove our words true.

HOW CAN WE BLESS THE JEWISH PEOPLE AT LARGE AS WELL AS BLESS THE JEWISH BELIEVERS IN JESUS?

Several years ago, I was asked to attend a large "Bless Israel" function. The event, to which leaders in the Jewish community were also invited, was sponsored by Christians. At the meeting I learned that one of the Christian speakers had just made a sizable monetary commitment to a well-known Jewish agency. When I heard this news, I was grieved and offended. *Lord, why?* I wondered. *Why could not some of this money have been given to some of the poor brothers and sisters in the Land? This brother loves Israel, but he obviously does not know what is going on among the believers!* I was not offended that he gave to the Jewish agency, since I believe that we are to bless Israel without regard to their faith in Messiah, but I also yearn for believers to be aware of their kinsmen in the faith among the Jewish people in the Land, many of whom are in need.

The more I thought about it, the angrier I became. Why can't Christians be more informed? This is an esteemed man of God, but he is not helping the situation. He is giving money—a lot of money—and none of it is going to the brothers in Yeshua!

Then I heard the quiet voice of God: "What if I told him to? What if I chose him for a different role? Maybe I told him to do that simply as a way of blessing My people and preparing them ultimately to accept Me."

"Forgive me, Lord," I prayed, resolving to leave such matters in greater hands.

At the same time, we Christians should become informed before we contribute to a ministry. Some of the best-advertised ministries may be producing very little fruit. Remember that Jesus said, "By their fruit you will recognize them" (Matt. 7:16). One very well-known organization has collected millions of dollars from evangelical believers all over the United States in the name of loving and blessing Israel, while only a small percentage of the money actually goes for its intended purpose. Some of it actually ends up in the hands of persecutors who actively harass Israel's Messianic believers. Let us seek the careful guidance and wisdom of the Lord and yet grow to be lavish in giving.

What do you have to say about Dual Covenant theology? Is it possible that the Jewish people today can come to the Father through the Mosaic covenant?

In an attempt to honor Jewish sensibilities, especially since the Holocaust, some theologians have decided that the Jewish people do not need Jesus. A few years ago, United States newscasters reported on a group of Christian leaders that issued a statement on this topic. The statement said that it is inappropriate to attempt to bring Jewish people to faith in Jesus as Messiah. "They already have a covenant with God," they seemed to be saying. "It is sufficient. They have no need of Jesus."

As much as we want to be sensitive to those who have been harassed, persecuted and killed by "Christians" for centuries, we cannot accept the Dual Covenant theory. Jesus came as Savior of both Jews and Gentiles. He spent His entire ministry time with His Jewish family. John's conclusion was that "[Jesus'] own did not receive him" (John 1:11). Paul, though specifically sent to the Gentiles, always took the gospel first to the Jews. Whole portions of the New Covenant Scriptures were written primarily to the Jewish people. Look at the opening lines of Peter's letters or James's epistle. Read the whole letter to the Hebrews, or consider the many times Matthew quotes the Old Testament in defense of his teaching.

Although we must walk lovingly with our Jewish friends, we will be doing them a gross disservice if we refuse to speak to them about their own Messiah, whom we have now received as our own. If we follow in the footsteps of one of the most famous rabbis in history, then we will say, "The longing of my heart and my prayer to God is that the Jewish people might be saved" (Rom. 10:1, *NLT*).

WHAT WILL HAPPEN TO THE JEWISH PEOPLE WHO DIED IN THE HOLOCAUST? SURELY YOU DO NOT BELIEVE THAT ALL OF THEM ARE LOST?

Rachmiel Frydland has written a very interesting book entitled *When Being Jewish Was a Crime*, which describes his years in Poland during the Nazi occupation. Rachmiel tells of his becoming a believer in Jesus during the Holocaust, as well as of others who came to faith, some of whom died during those years of horror. Not only does this remind us that we never know all the facts and therefore cannot render judgment on anyone, but it also gives us hope for all those seekers after God who have suffered unjustly.

Luke describes the final hours of Jesus' life, when, with a last gasp, He grants salvation to one of the men hanging on the cross beside Him (see Luke 23:39-43). I rest in the faith that those of every generation who seek the Lord will find Him.

HOW SHOULD WE RESPOND TO THOSE WHO BELIEVE THAT GOD IS FINISHED WITH ISRAEL?

I tell people that we must not be angry with those who believe today what we believed last week! Let us pray for revelation. Remember that God Himself must open eyes and hearts (see Luke 24:31; Acts 16:14).

One of my rabbi friends relates some rather pointed anti-Jewish conversations he had while teaching at a Roman Catholic seminary. As the discussion became more and more heated, the amiable rabbi stepped over to the wall of the classroom, took the crucifix from the wall, held it to his heart and said quite loudly,

"Dear Jesus, we are not welcome here!"

For centuries the Church has insisted that Jewish believers in Jesus surrender their Jewish identity and become assimilated into the strange (to a Jewish person) culture of the Gentiles. Paul attempted to correct that thinking with his Roman letter, in which he repeatedly asserts that God is not finished with Israel and that eventually all of Israel will be saved. Early Christian theologians paid little attention to Paul's admonition and soon began to demand that Jewish believers forsake their heritage if they were to become "Christian," a Greek name the early Jewish believers never would have given to themselves.

In the last few centuries, some among both Christians and Jews began to believe that the Jewish nation would soon come to faith. Among the strongest advocates for the return of the Jewish nation to the Land and for their acknowledgment of Jesus as Messiah were the early Puritans.[3] On the Jewish side, one of the earliest "Messianic Jews," who insisted that his baptism into the Name of Yeshua did not drown his Jewishness and that he was indeed still a Jew, was Rabbi Joseph Rabinowitz, who came to faith in the late nineteenth century. For almost two decades he was the spiritual leader of a vibrant congregation of Jewish believers, a congregation that after his death did not survive into the twentieth century.[4]

In light of the recent Messianic Jewish movement, in which hundreds of thousands of Jewish people have come to faith in Jesus as Messiah—many of whom continue in their Jewish practices—the doctrine that Gentile believers have replaced the Jewish people as recipients of salvation and God's covenant promises is losing ground. Theologians who believe that the Jewish people will be saved after the Gentile part of the Church is taken away have been forced to rethink their doctrinal position.

The truth that Jesus is Jewish had until recently become so veiled to parts of the Church that some Christians have actually been shocked when they have been reminded of His Jewishness. Interestingly, one people group in the world has no doubt. Militant Islam is very aware that Jesus is Jewish and that there is an eternal connection between Israel and the Church. Friday sermons in mosques are often saturated with anti-Jewish and anti-Christian rhetoric. One such sermon included this clarion cry to Allah: "Oh, Allah, finish off our enemies, who are enemies of our religion! The Jews and their friends, the Christians, are our enemies. Let the ground shake under the feet of the Jews. Put fear into the hearts of Jews and Christians, and let their blood freeze in their veins."[5] Islam's greatest fear is that God is not yet finished with Israel and that He will continue to sustain her.

WHY DO YOU ADVOCATE THAT WE NOT USE THE VERB "CONVERT" WHEN WE SPEAK OF JEWISH PEOPLE COMING TO FAITH? DOES "CONVERT" NOT MEAN "TURN"? AND IS THAT NOT EXACTLY WHAT THEY HAVE DONE?

A few months ago, as I walked into a local bakery, I was greeted by three women who were sitting at a nearby table. Two of the women were from the temple; one was from my home congregation. They motioned for me to come over. As I neared their table, one of the Jewish ladies mischievously asked, "Are you trying to convert all the Jews?"

"Oh, no!" I lightheartedly responded. "I just want you to recognize your own Messiah! You are the ones who have kept alive this faith in the one true God. If it had not been for you, we would all still be worshiping sticks and stones!"

Yes, in the strictest sense of the word, each of us, whether Jew or non-Jew, converts when we come to God through Yeshua. The apostle Paul, a Jew, converted when he became a believer.

There is, however, another sense in which Jewish people, who have been the carriers of faith in God, do *not* convert or turn; they simply *return* to the faith of their fathers. They begin to believe their own Scriptures (which we Gentiles have inherited from them). They acknowledge their own Messiah.

If that in itself does not seem to be sufficient grounds to avoid the word "convert," let me tell you why I personally avoid it. It's because for centuries the Church demanded that when Jewish people came to faith in Jesus, they had to give up being "Jewish" and instead become absorbed into the Gentile Christian world. Such assimilation, if completely successful, would result in the annihilation of the Jewish race—which was in no way the intention of the early apostles and believers, as Scripture and history abundantly document.

A further reason for not speaking of Jewish "conversions" is the imagery that this word evokes in a Jewish mind. The word harkens back to times when the Church forced conversions, when Jewish children would be taken from their families, forcefully baptized and then given over to "Christian" families, since the children had become "Christians" and required a "Christian" rearing.

WHY DO JEWISH BELIEVERS RARELY REFER TO "CHRIST"?

The first believers in Jesus were Jewish, as we know; and if they were Hebrew-speakers, they would have referred to Jesus by His Hebrew name, Yeshua, and by the Hebrew word meaning "Anointed One," Mashiach (Messiah) rather than by the Greek names *Iesous* (Jesus) and Christos (Christ). Since the New

Testament manuscripts were written in Greek, it seems natural for us to speak of "Jesus" and of "Christ." In an attempt to put the message back into its original context, however, our believing Jewish brothers and sisters, and even many of us who walk closely with them, refer to Him as "Messiah" rather than "Christ," sometimes even when reading Scripture aloud.

WHY DO THE JEWISH PEOPLE NOT REFER TO THEIR CONGREGATION AS A CHURCH? IS THAT ALSO JUST CULTURAL?

To Jewish believers the word "church," like the words "Christ," "Christian" and "convert," brings up images of gas chambers, pogroms, the Inquisition and the Crusades, through which millions of Jewish people have suffered and died. Jewish gatherings, whether Messianic or more traditional, choose rather to refer to themselves as "congregations," perhaps even as "synagogues."

Remember, also, that the term "Jew" can be offensive and may sound as if the Jewish person is becoming bait for persecution. The word "Jewish" is much kinder and more appropriate. You will notice that I rarely use the term "Jews," but rather "Jewish people."

WHAT ARE SOME SIMPLE GUIDELINES FOR A CHURCH THAT IS BEGINNING TO UNDERSTAND THE JEWISH CONNECTION AND WANTS TO BE SENSITIVE TO JEWISH BELIEVERS?

Since I myself have been the pastor of a church, I have had a number of years to ponder this question. The last chapter in *Your People Shall Be My People* addressed this matter, but I am not satisfied with those answers. I would like to offer some additional suggestions:

1. *Challenge your people to be Romans 11:11 believers.* Romans 11:11 believers are so full of the Lord that they radiate love, goodness and compassion, making everyone who does not know Jesus as Messiah— whether Jewish or non-Jewish—*jealous.* One of my young Israeli brothers brought us a strong challenge the other night by referring to Moses' conversation with God after being called to lead Israel out of Egypt and through the desert. "If your Presence does not go with us, do not send us up from here," Moses said. "How will anyone know that you are pleased with me and with your people unless you go with us? What else will distinguish me and your people from all the other people on the face of the earth?" (Exod. 33:15,16). The distinguishing mark of true believers is the radiance of God that comes from His presence within them. My young brother then pointed us to Moses' habit of putting a veil over his face as the glory of God began to fade so that Israel would not see the glory of His presence as it grew fainter (see Exod. 34:33-35; 2 Cor. 3:13). One of the great liabilities of many believers today is that we have substituted all sorts of veils to disguise the fact that we are not living in the presence of the Lord and that we are not radiating His likeness. Challenge your people to be God-indwelt, loving, forgiving, compassionate people, who are not swayed by the circumstances of life nor even by those who mistreat them, but who glow with the Presence.

2. *Restore to your church its relationship to the Jewish faith and the Jewish people.* Become aware of the biblical calendar and sufficiently informed about the biblical diet so that you don't end up hosting a big dinner, serving ham, shrimp or lobster, on one of the high holy days of Israel and thereby unintentionally offending your Jewish guests.

3. *Seek the heart of the Lord on ways to bless the descendants of Abraham.* When you do, you and your congregation come under the full blessing assured in the original promise to Abraham (see Gen. 12:1-3). The experience of Pastor Ron Johnson (see chapter 6) is similar to the experiences of many of us who have found ways to bless Abraham's descendants. For example, if you visit Israel, either individually or with a group, do not just tour the Land; rather, take time for the people. And most important, arrange to meet some of your covenant brothers and sisters of faith. Take them gifts. Pack extra luggage with humanitarian aid items for the poor. Be a participant with God in what He is doing in our day.

4. *Prioritize the Jewish people in your church's outreach,* remembering that we have accepted their Messiah and desire them to come to know Him as well (see Rom. 1:16). Invite a Jewish believer to explain to the people in your church ways in which they can be sensitive to the heritage of the Jewish people and the history of the Church as they, nonetheless, share the gospel of the Messiah with their Jewish friends. Find those clear references to Jesus in the Hebrew Scriptures for use in conversations, giving yourself to genuine friendship, not simply "targeting" people for

a superficial presentation of the gospel. Remember that the Jewish people have been the object of conversion efforts for 19 centuries, even at the point of the sword. It is time for authentic, respectful, heart-rooted sharing of faith in Yeshua, making abundantly clear that Jewish followers of Jesus do not become Gentile Christians, but rather enter the deepest relationship with the God of Israel through their Messiah, who was promised by the prophets.

5. *Pray Isaiah 62:6-7 and Psalm 122:6 prayers,* according to the pattern of Daniel, Ezra and Nehemiah. "You who call on the LORD, give yourselves no rest, and give him no rest till he establishes Jerusalem and makes her the praise of the earth," says Isaiah (Isa. 62:6-7). "Pray for the peace of Jerusalem," cries the psalmist (Ps. 122:6). "We have sinned and done wrong," Daniel intercedes, weeping (Dan. 9:5). "Our guilt has reached to the heavens," echoes Ezra, in a Daniel-type prayer (Ezra 9:6). "I confess the sins we Israelites, including myself and my father's house, have committed against you," agrees Nehemiah (Neh. 1:6). Lead your people in intercessory confession of the sins of the church, of your city and of the nation.

6. *Obey Romans 15:27, Galatians 6:10 and Acts 20:35 with your gifts,* both personally and congregationally, prioritizing Israel, giving special emphasis to the family of faith and never neglecting the poor. Look for ministries that are producing fruit (see Matt. 7:16) by considering these questions: Where are Jewish people coming to faith? Where are the poor being supported? Who is seeking to help Jewish people return to the Land? Are the leaders of the ministries men and

women of humility and integrity? If you do not personally know about the ministries, then rely on your brothers and sisters whom you respect and who do know them. Great expenditures may produce little help. Give generously, even lavishly, but wisely. If you need help, check out some of the ministries mentioned in appendix C or at our website: www.caleb company.com. These lists are by no means definitive, but they are a place to begin. The ministries listed are led by your brothers and sisters who are determined to see the kingdom birthed in Israel. I have believed for some time that every church throughout the world that establishes right order for Jewish ministry will come into a greater blessing in the Lord. One of the ways that could happen would be for every congregation, no matter what its specific calling in regard to world missions, to tithe its mission budget into Jewish ministry.

7. *Be ready to help Jewish people in the Diaspora return to the Land of their inheritance.* "I will beckon to the Gentiles, I will lift up my banner to the peoples; they will bring your sons in their arms and carry your daughters on their shoulders," Isaiah predicted (Isa. 49:22). Indeed, many of the ships and much of the finances for the return of Israel out of their exile has come from the nations. This return will not be complete until all are "home" (see Ezek. 39:28).

8. *Pray that Isaiah 6, Hosea 3:4-5 and Ezekiel 37:6 revelation will come to all of Israel.* Isaiah saw a time when Israel's eyes would be open. Hosea referred to the last days, in which Israel would come trembling to the Lord. Ezekiel predicted that Israel would come to know the

Lord during the time of her return from the nations. On the basis of these Scriptures, know and pray with confidence that Jewish eyes will be opened to their Messiah.

9. *Pray with faith for the Romans 11:12,15 and Ezekiel 36:23 revival to sweep the earth.* Paul sees "greater riches" and "life from the dead" coming to the whole world when Israel begins to come back. Ezekiel prophesies about this revival that "then the nations will know that I am the LORD." Know that this is the time for world revival so that we can pray and act accordingly.

10. *Become a part of the Ephesians 2:15 "one new man" body of believers.* This "one new man" is comprised of both Jews and Gentiles from all the nations, each with their own distinctive culture and heritage, who live together and who love and encourage one another.

WHAT IF OUR MINISTRY IS PRIMARILY TO THE NATIONS? WE CANNOT ALL BE INVOLVED IN JEWISH MINISTRY.

Recently I taught in Youth With A Mission's (YWAM) School of Jewish Studies at their University of the Nations (U of N) campus in Kona, Hawaii. I went at the invitation of a very gifted woman from our home congregation; she heads up YWAM's Jewish World Office and was leading the school. I was not prepared for the impact those few days were to have on me.

YWAM is now the largest mission organization in the world, and their U of N campus in Kona is the hub of the university, where 40 nations are represented at any given time. Sister campuses are scattered across the globe. On the first Monday morning of my visit, I was a part of a worship time in which young people from many nations were invited to come forward and pray in their native languages. As I stood on the university's grounds in Kona, thoughts from Paul's Roman letter came flooding in on me again: *First for the Jew. Greater riches to the nations when the Jews come home. Life from the dead. Owe it to the Jews. Remember the poor.* I suddenly felt myself in the bosom of world evangelism, and I knew that the message I carry about God's heart for Israel and the Jewish people must spread to every missionary in the world.

EVERY GENTILE CHRISTIAN WHOSE HEART BEGINS TO OPEN TO THIS "PARENT" PEOPLE OF OUR FAITH IS A VERIFICATION OF THE WORDS OF THE PROPHETS AND IS A DELIGHT.

Oh, that mission agencies would establish God's priorities—first to the Jewish people in whatever nation of their calling and then to the Gentiles! And how I long for mission agencies to understand the impact that all this will have on world evangelism! Faith for the effectiveness of every evangelistic work will be enlarged as we recognize the words of the prophets.

No, we cannot all be involved in Jewish ministry, but we can all have a heart for this closest blood family of Jesus. We can stand confidently on His Word, which says that their eyes will be opened to Him! Standing with the prophets will enhance all of our callings.

We live to see His kingdom birthed among His covenant people and among the nations. We throb with hope and pulsate with anticipation. Every new believer among the people of Israel is cause for incomparable joy. Every Gentile Christian whose heart begins to open to this "parent" people of faith is a verification of the words of the prophets and is a delight. Our hearing of the gospel spreading to the nations brings a rush of elation. To see Jew and Gentile, Jew and Arab, affectionately embrace in the common love of Messiah is like water to our thirsty souls. For this we live and to this we were born. "I have no greater joy," said the aged apostle John, "than to hear that my children are walking in the truth" (3 John 4).

"O Israel, put your hope in the LORD, for with the LORD is unfailing love and with him is full redemption," we cry with the psalmist, before confidently declaring, "He himself will redeem Israel from all their sins" (Ps. 130:7,8).

With the people of Israel, we say of Jerusalem, "her stones are dear to your servants; her very dust moves them to pity. [Yes,] [t]he nations will [indeed yet come to] fear the name of the LORD, [yes,] all the kings of the earth will revere your glory" (Ps. 102:14-15).

"You will arise and have compassion on Zion," we say, with great faith in Father God, "for it is time to show favor to her; *the appointed time has come!*" (Ps. 102:13, emphasis added).

Notes

1. See chapter 6, endnote 3, for a description of this council.
2. Ray Waddle, "Rabbi Offended by Pastor's Remarks," *The Tennessean*, April 18, 1997, p. 1.
3. The name "Puritans" was used first in the sixteenth century in referring to a group of reformers who sought to "purify" the Anglican Church. See appendix B for quotations from some of these Christian leaders.
4. The Rabinowitz story can be found in Kai Kjaer-Hansen's book, *The Herzl of Jewish Christianity: Joseph Rabinowitz and the Messianic Movement* (Grand Rapids, MI: Wm. B. Eerdmans Publishing Co., 1995).
5. "Friday Sermons Incite the Arab Masses," *Israel Today*, September 2002, p. 9.

SUGGESTED BIBLE READING PLAN

Let me encourage you, even if you are a pastor or a Bible teacher, to have a Bible reading plan for your own personal growth—a plan that has nothing to do with the sermons or lessons you prepare, one that will insure that you read through the entire Bible with the desire to learn more for yourself. Read, asking the Holy Spirit for more understanding and insight. This approach to Bible reading will affect your sermons and teaching, of course, but it is not done with that intention.

Many of us, even pastors and leaders, have begun all sorts of systematic reading schemes, only to cast them aside after a few weeks. This is often because we get behind, grow discouraged or feel guilty about the failure, and we give up on the plan altogether. Others of us may do hours of Bible study and reading, but we have no consistent plan to be sure that we read the entire Bible regularly.

For this reason I suggest a method in which you are never ahead, but also never behind, a method by which you read in various sections of the Bible at the same time and become your own best cross-reference.

The plan I have used for years divides the Bible into five parts:

1. Genesis through Esther—the historical section of the Hebrew Scripture;[1]
2. Job through Song of Solomon—the poetic portion;

3. Isaiah through Malachi—the Prophets;
4. Matthew through Acts—the Gospels and Acts;
5. Romans through Revelation—the letters and the prophecy of John.

I read from one Bible, making a small number denoting the year, as I move forward in each of the sections (6 for 2006, 7 for 2007 and so on). I may read in five different places on any given day. I often begin in the Psalms and then go to the Prophets; then on to the Gospels or Acts, to the letters or John's Revelation, and back to the historical section of the Old Testament.

Each of the sections, with the exception of the latter, is finished in less than a year by reading one chapter a day. You may proceed, however, as slowly or as swiftly as you like. You will never be behind, and the plan will work for you for the rest of your life. Just choose the Bible you want to use and begin today. In this way you will not be neglecting some portion of Scripture that may hold great benefits for you.

Note

1. If you would like to read the same passages from the Torah that are being read in the synagogues each Sabbath, you may want to reserve Genesis through Deuteronomy for Saturday reading, leaving Joshua through Esther as the portion of the historical section that you read during the week.

APPENDIX B

QUOTATIONS FROM PAST GENERATIONS OF THE SAINTS ON ISRAEL AND THE JEWISH PEOPLE

The following quotations, taken from Iain H. Murray's *The Puritan Hope: Revival and the Interpretation of Prophecy* (Carlisle, PA: The Banner of Truth Trust, 1971, reprinted in 1998), chronicle some of the expectations of the Jewish return that began to surface about 450 years ago (the page numbers listed are from Murray's book):

Geneva Bible, 1560. Marginal notes on Romans 11:26: "He sheweth that the time shall come that the whole nation of the Jews, though not every one particularly, shall be joined to the church of Christ" (p. 41).

Comment on Romans 11:15: "The [Jews] now remain, as it were, in death for lack of the Gospel, but when both they and the Gentiles shall embrace Christ, the world shall be restored to a new life" (p. 72).

William Perkins, 1579, Christ's College, Cambridge. "The Lord saith, *All the nations shall be blessed in Abraham*; Hence I gather that the nation of the Jews shall be called, and converted to the participation of this blessing; when, and how, God knows: but that it shall be done before the end of the world we know" (p. 42).

Elnathan Parr, in his exposition of Romans, the *Plain Exposition*, published in 1620: "The casting off of the Jews, was our Calling; but the Calling of the Jews shall not be our casting off, but our greater enriching in grace, and that two ways: First, in regard of the company of believers, when the thousands of Israel shall come in, which shall doubtless cause many Gentiles which now lie in ignorance, error and doubt, to receive the Gospel and join with them. The world shall then be a golden world, rich in golden men, saith Ambrose. Secondly, in respect of the graces, which shall then in more abundance be rained down upon the Church" (p. 46).

John Owens, speaking before the House of Commons in 1649, spoke of "the bringing home of his ancient people to be one fold with the fullness of the Gentiles . . . in answer to millions of prayers put up at the throne of grace, for this very glory, in all generations" (p. 100).

John Brown, *Exposition of Romans*, 1666. Iain Murray's preface to Brown's comments on Romans 11:12: "In verse 12, Brown says, the apostle meets a difficulty which might arise in the minds of Gentiles following the disclosure of verse 11 that the hardening of the Jews was not the final dispensation of God toward them. If room has been made in God's kingdom by the casting out of the jews, the thought might occur that the restoration of the jews would lead to the Gentiles being cast out."

Brown's comments on Romans 11:12: "To this the apostle answereth, that, on the contrary, the Gentiles shall have braver days then, than ever they had; for *if their fall* or stumbling was the occasion by which the Gentiles dispersed up and down the world, enjoyed the riches of the gospel and of the knowledge of God in Christ, and their diminishing (to the same purpose, and explicating what is meant by *their fall)* that is, their rejecting of the [Messiah] for the most part, so as there were but few behind, and that nation was worn to a thin company and a small number of such as embraced the gospel, *be the riches of the Gentiles,* the same with *the riches of the world; how much more shall their abundance be?* That is, How much more shall their inbringing and fullness, or the conversion of the body and bulk of that nation (for it is opposed to their diminishing) tend to the enriching of the Gentile world in the knowledge of Christ; and so the Gentiles need not fear that the conversion of the Jews shall any way prejudice them; but they may expect to reap advantage thereby" (pp. 66-67).

Brown's comments on Romans 11:15: "Will there not be joyful days thro' the world, and among the Gentiles, when they shall be received into favour again? Will it not be like the resurrection from the dead, when Jew and Gentile shall both enjoy the same felicity and happiness? Seeing out of the dead state of the Jews, when cast without doors, God brought life to the Gentiles, will he not much more do so out of their enlivened estate. [W]ill it not be to the Gentiles as resurrection from the dead?" (pp. 67-68).

Robert Leighton, in a sermon on Isaiah 60:1 delivered in January 1642: "Undoubtedly, that people of the Jews shall once more be commanded to *arise* and *shine,* and their return shall be *the riches of the Gentiles* (Rom. 11:12), and that shall be a more glorious time than ever the Church of God did yet behold" (p. 75).

Samuel Rutherford, 1633, in a letter to Lady Jane Kenmure from Anwoth: "O to see the sight, next to Christ's Coming in the clouds, the most joyful! Our elder brethren the Jews and Christ fall upon one another's necks and kiss each other! They have been long asunder; they will be kind to one another when they meet. O day! O longed-for and lovely day-dawn! O sweet Jesus, let me see that sight which will be as life from the dead, thee and thy ancient people in mutual embraces" (p. 98).

Increase Mather, *The Mystery of Israel's Salvation Explained and Applied,* 1669. "That there shall be a general conversion of the Tribes of Israel is a truth which in some measure hath been known and believed in all ages of the Church of God, since the Apostles' days . . . Only in these late days, these things obtained credit much more universally than heretofore" (p. 45).

James Durham, 1680. "Whatever may be doubted of their restoring to their land, yet they shall be brought to a visible Church-state. Not only in particular persons here and there in congregations; but that multitudes, yes, the whole body of them shall be brought, in a common way with the Gentiles, to profess Christ, which cannot be denied, as Romans 11 is clear and that will be enough to satisfy us" (p. 61).

John Albert Bengel (1687-1752). Regarding Bengel's commentary on Romans 11:12 and 25, Iain Murray stated: "All such obstacles to the incoming of the Gentiles 'will be broken through at the proper time,' and when an abundance (Bengel's interpretation of '[fullness]' in Romans 11:12 and 25) of the Gentiles have been converted, the hardening of Israel will terminate'. The full conversion of Israel will then lead to the wider blessing of the world" (p. 132).

Thomas Boston, in a sermon in 1716 entitled "Encouragement to Pray for the Conversion of the Jews": "Are you longing for a revival to the churches, now lying like dry bones, would you fain have the Spirit of life enter into them? Then pray for the Jews. For if the casting away of them be the reconciling of the world; what shall the receiving of them be, but life from the dead? . . . That will be a lively time, a time of a great outpouring of the Spirit, that will carry reformation to a greater height than yet has been" (p. 114).

Jonathan Edwards (1703-1758). "Though we do not know the time in which this conversion of Israel will come to pass, yet thus much we may determine by Scripture, that it will be before the glory of the Gentile part of the church shall be fully accomplished, because it is said that their coming in shall be life from the dead to the Gentiles" (Rom. 11:12,15) (p. 154).

Charles Simeon, early nineteenth century, at a missionary meeting, seemed so carried away with the future of the Jews that a friend passed him a slip of paper with the question: "'Six millions of Jews and six hundred millions of Gentiles—which is the most important?' Simeon at once scribbled back: 'If the conversion of the six is to be life from the dead to the six hundred, what then?'" (p. 155).

Charles H. Spurgeon, 1855, in a volume of sermons: "I think we do not attach sufficient importance to the restoration of the Jews. We do not think enough of it. But certainly, if there is anything promised in the Bible, it is this . . . The day shall yet come when the Jews, who were the first apostles to the Gentiles, the first missionaries to us who were afar off, shall be gathered in again. Until that shall be, the fullness of the church's glory can never come. Matchless benefits to the world are bound up with the restoration of Israel, their gathering in shall be life from the dead" (p. 256).

Contact Information for Ministries Mentioned

The following are websites and contact persons for the ministries mentioned in this book:

Beit Asaph Congregation
Netanya, Israel
Evan and Maala Thomas
http://www.beit-asaph.org.il

Beit Immanuel Congregation
Jaffa, Israel
David and Michaela Lazarus
http://www.beitimmanuel.org/

Dugit Messianic Outreach Center
Tel Aviv, Israel
Avi and Chaya Mizrachi
http://www.dugit.org

El-Roii Congregation
Ofer and Chris Amitai
Jerusalem, Israel
E-Mail: elroii@zahav.net.il

Final Frontier Ministries
Omer (Beersheva), Israel
Avner and Rachel Boskey
http://www.davidstent.org

Gateways Beyond International
Cyprus
David and Emma Rudolph
http://gatewaysbeyond.org

Heart Rock
Jerusalem, Israel
Ayal (Richard) and Yardena Frieden
http://www.heartrock.org

International Christian Embassy Jerusalem
Jerusalem, Israel
Malcolm Hedding
http://www.icej.org/

Jerusalem House of Prayer
Jerusalem, Israel
Tom Hess
http://www.jhopfan.org/index.asp

Kehilat HaCarmel
Haifa, Israel
David and Karen Davis
http://www.carmel-assembly.org.il/

King of Kings Congregation
Jerusalem, Israel
Wayne and Anne Hilsden
http://www.kokaradio.com/

Maoz Ministry
Tel Aviv, Israel
Ari and Shira Sorko-Ram
http://www.maozisrael.org

Revive Israel
Jerusalem, Israel
Asher (Keith) and Betty Intrater
http://www.revive-israel.org

Tents of Mercy
Kiriyat Yam, Israel
Eitan (Andrew) and Connie Shishkoff
http://www.tents-of-mercy.org

Tikkun Ministries
Gaithersburg, Maryland
and Jerusalem, Israel
Dan and Patti Juster
http://www.tikkunministries.org

Toward Jerusalem Council II
Dallas, Texas
Marty Waldman
http://www.tjcii.org

RECOMMENDED READING

Aikman, David. *Jesus in Beijing: How Christianity Is Transforming China and Changing the Global Balance of Power.* Washington, D.C.: Regenery Publishing, Inc., 2003.

Chernoff, Yohanna. *Born a Jew . . . Die a Jew: The Story of Martin Chernoff, a Pioneer in Messianic Judaism.* Hagerstown, MD: EBED Publications, 1996.

Danyun. *Lilies Amongst Thorns: Chinese Christians Tell Their Story Through Blood and Tears.* Translated by Brother Dennis. Kent, England: Sovereign World, 1991.

Frydland, Rachmiel. *When Being Jewish Was a Crime.* Nashville: Thomas Nelson Publishers, Inc., 1978.

Garrison, David. *Church Planting Movements: How God Is Redeeming a Lost World.* Midlothian, VA: WIGTake Resources, 2004.

Goll, James W. *Praying for Israel's Destiny: Effective Intercession for God's Purposes in the Middle East.* Grand Rapids, MI: Chosen Books, 2005.

Hattaway, Paul. *The Heavenly Man: The Remarkable True Story of Chinese Christian Brother Yun.* London: Monarch Books, 2003.

Intrater, Keith [Asher]. *From Iraq to Armageddon: The Final Showdown Approaches.* Shippensburg, PA: Destiny Image Publishers, 2003.

Israel's Restoration (newsletter). Gaithersburg, MD: Tikkun Ministries, n.d.

Jenkins, Phillip. *The Next Christendom: The Coming of Global Christianity*. New York: Oxford University Press, 2002.

Juster, Dan. *Jewish Roots: A Foundation of Biblical Theology*. Shippensburg, PA: Destiny Image, 1995.

_____. *One People Many Tribes: A Primer on Church History from a Messianic Jewish Perspective*. Clarence, NY: Kairos Publishing, 1999.

_____. *The Irrevocable Calling*. Gaithersburg, MD: Tikkun Ministries, 1996.

Kjaer-Hansen, Kai and Bodil F. Skjott, eds. *Facts and Myths About the Messianic Congregations in Israel*. Jerusalem, Israel: United Christian Council in Israel in cooperation with the Caspari Center for Biblical and Jewish Studies, 1999.

Kjaer-Hansen, Kai. *Joseph Rabinowitz and the Messianic Movement: The Herzl of Jewish Christianity*. Grand Rapids, MI: Eerdmans Publishing Co., 1995.

Lightle, Steve. *Exodus II: Let My People Go*. Kingwood, TX: Hunter Books, 1983.

Rutz, James, *Megashift: Igniting Spiritual Power*. Colorado Springs, CO: Empowerment Press, 2005.

Stern, David H. *Complete Jewish Bible: An English Version of the*

Tanakh (Old Testament) and B'rit Hadashah (New Testament). Clarksville, MD: Jewish New Testament Publications, 1988.

The Messianic Times: Serving the International Messianic Jewish Community. Niagara Falls, NY: Times of the Messiah Ministries, n.d.

Wagner, C. Peter and Joseph Thompson. *Out of Africa: How the Spiritual Explosion Among Nigerians Is Impacting the World.* Ventura, CA: Regal Books, 2004.

THE CALEB COMPANY

The Caleb Company is a nonprofit organization named after Israel's famous warrior who was still taking mountains in his old age and whose descendants were to inherit the Land (see Num. 14:24; Josh. 14:11). The Caleb Company was formed to further the kingdom of God through encouraging pastors and young leaders, supporting and challenging the Church to recognize the growing movement of God in Israel and among the Jewish people, and helping unite Jew and Gentile together in Messiah Yeshua though the following ways:

- Supporting Jewish believers, especially those in the Land (this includes helping to raise financial and practical support as well as taking a role in restoration and reconciliation)
- Helping the Church come alive to its Jewish/Hebrew roots (this happens primarily through Don's or others' speaking to pastors and leaders, both nationally and internationally)
- Empowering and mentoring others, especially in their part of the "Israel Mandate" (this is accomplished by establishing relational connections, partnering with others in The Caleb Company family and gathering and shipping relevant materials)
- Being a bridge between the believers in the Land and believers in the nations so that we may participate together for His purposes in our day

Don Finto is the founder of The Caleb Company; however, this ministry is not about just one man (except Yeshua Ha Mashiach, Jesus the Messiah). We encourage you to search the Scriptures for yourself and discover more about God and His heart. We exist to exalt the God of Abraham, Isaac and Jacob and to see His Holy Spirit move in and through us to work His will (that is, to see His kingdom come here on the earth as it is in heaven). This is our inheritance, this is our legacy, and we encourage you to join us in the pilgrimage.

If you find the message of this book intriguing or want to know more, you may contact us at the following:

The Caleb Company
Don Finto
68 Music Square East
Nashville, TN 37203
www.calebcompany.com

Also from Don Finto

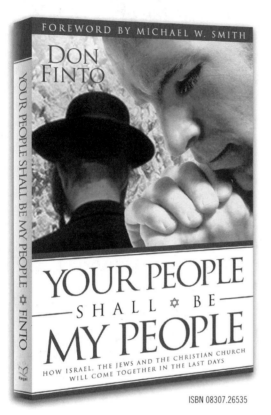